WORLD
RELIGIONS

· EXPLORING HISTORY ·

WORLD
RELIGIONS

·

Discover the religions that have
shaped world history

· SIMON ADAMS ·

LORENZ BOOKS

First published in 2000 by Lorenz Books

© Anness Publishing Limited 2000

Lorenz Books is an imprint of
Anness Publishing Limited
Hermes House
88-89 Blackfriars Road
London SE1 8HA

This edition distributed in Canada by
Raincoast Books
8680 Cambie Street
Vancouver
British Columbia V6P 6M9

A CIP catalogue record for this book is available from the
British Library

Publisher: Joanna Lorenz
Managing Editor: Gilly Cameron Cooper
Senior Editor: Lisa Miles

Produced by Miles Kelly Publishing Limited
The Bardfield Centre,
Great Bardfield, Essex CM7 4SL
Publishing Director: Jim Miles
Editorial Director: Paula Borton
Art Director: Clare Sleven
Project Management: Neil de Cort
Project Editor: Clare Oliver
Editorial Assistant: Simon Nevill
Design: Sally Boothroyd
Cover Design: Jo Brewer
Art Commissioning: Natasha Smith, Susanne Grant
Picture Research: Kate Miles; Janice Bracken
Lesley Cartlidge; Liberty Mella

The author wishes to thank Susan Malyan for her help in
preparing the spreads on Judaism and Christianity.

The publishers would like to thank the following
artists who have contributed to this book:
Vanessa Card; Terry Gabbey (AFA); Sally Holmes; Peter Sarson; Rob
Sheffield; Mike White (Temple Rogers); Roger Gorringe (Illustration
Ltd.); Terry Riley Studio; Peter Gregory; Clive Spong (Linden
Artists); Sally Holmes; .Ross Watton (SGA); Chris Odgers;
Chris Forsey; Sally Holmes; Catherine Ward.
Maps: Steve Sweet & Stuart Squires (SGA).

Main Maps: Roger Stewart.

The publishers wish to thank the following
for supplying photographs for this book:
Page 13 (BC) Judy McCaskey; 16 (BC) Kaveh Kazemi/ Panos
Pictures; 21 (TR) Victoria and Albert Museum/ The Bridgeman Art
Library; 23 (TL) Lindsay Hebberd/ CORBIS; 24 (BR) The National
Museum of India/ The Bridgeman Art Library; 27 (TR) The
Bridgeman Art Library; 29 (BL) Alain le Garsmeur/ Panos Pictures;
33 (TR) Bennett Dean: Eye Ubiquitous/ CORBIS; 34 (CR) Dinodia
Picture Agency, Bombay/ The Bridgeman Art Library, (BC) Charles
& Josette Lenars/ CORBIS; Earl & Nazima Kowall/ CORBIS; 40 (C)
Clare Oliver; 41 (TR, BC) Clare Oliver; 42 (BR) Daniel Lainé/
CORBIS; 46 (BR) David H. Wells/ CORBIS; 47 (CR) Dave Bartruff/
CORBIS; 51 (BC) Kevin Fleming/ CORBIS; 53 (BC) The Bridgeman
Art Library; 54 (BR) Piers Benatar/ Panos Pictures; 55 (BC) Sonia
Halliday Photographs; 56 (TR) Bettmann/ CORBIS; 57 (TR) Sonia
Halliday Photographs; 58 (BL) Robert Leslie; 59 (TL) CORBIS; 60
(TL) Bettmann/CORBIS; (CR) Lake County Museum/ CORBIS; 61
(TL) Bettmann/ CORBIS, (BR) Denis O'Regan/ CORBIS.

All other pictures from
Dover Publications and Miles Kelly archives.

Printed and bound in Singapore
3 5 7 9 10 8 6 4 2

CONTENTS

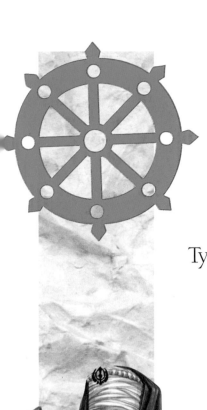

Introduction

▲ OHM SYMBOL
Every religion has its own symbol. This identifies the religion and its believers. Hindus use the Ohm symbol. Jews have the menorah (candlestick), Christians have the cross and Muslims use the hilal (crescent moon and star).

▼ KEY DATES
The panel below charts the history of religion, from the earliest religion of the ancient Egyptians to the new religions founded during the 1900s.

THROUGHOUT HUMAN HISTORY, people have asked questions about life and their place in the world. They have wondered why evil and suffering exist, how the world came into existence and how it might end. Above all, they have asked if there is a god who guides and directs the world, or whether events just roll on for ever without purpose or end.

There is no definite answer to these questions, but people have tried to make sense of their lives through religion. The first religions, such as Hinduism, were pantheistic, that is they involved the worship of many gods. With Judaism, a new type of religion known as monotheism (the worship of a single god) began. Christianity and Islam are also monotheistic religions.

At first sight the teachings of the various religions appear to be very different. In fact, they can be placed into two main groups. The first group includes Hinduism and Buddhism. These religions state that the world is a spiritual place, and that it is possible to escape the endless circle of birth, death and rebirth and reach a totally spiritual life. The second group includes Christianity and Islam. These religions say that the world is essentially good, but that humans make it bad. They urge people to behave well in order to change the world and make it a better place.

All the various religions use similar techniques to put across their messages. They tell stories and myths to explain complicated subjects in a way that is easy to understand. They use symbols that identify the faith and its believers and they use rituals, such as

▲ THE GOSPELS
All religions have their own holy book or books. These contain the words of God or the gods, as told to his earthly prophets (messengers). Jews have the Torah, Christians have the Bible, Sikhs have the Guru Granth Sahib and Muslims have the Qur'an. Many religions also have books of religious laws, such as the Jewish Talmud.

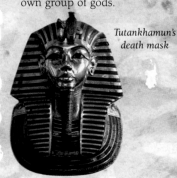

Christian baptism. Finally, religions develop societies that bind believers together. These techniques help worshippers to understand their faith and apply it in their daily lives.

Examining the development of the world's religions is one way to chart the history of humankind. Holy scriptures are the oldest written records we have. Not all the information contained in them need be read as historical fact. However, the latest archaeological discoveries are proving that many stories in the religious texts are based on true events.

At the start of the third millennium AD, the majority of the world's population follow a religion. There are also people, known as agnostics, who are not convinced that there is a god, but do not rule the possibility out. Atheists are people who do not believe in the existence of any god at all. Some people worship nature, while others, known as humanists, believe in the supremacy of human beings and their ability to make sensible decisions for themselves.

◀ A PHYSICAL GOD
Many religions see a human as a form, or manifestation, of their god on earth. Egyptians thought this way about their pharaoh, and some Chinese religions thought that the Emperor (left) was also a god.

▲ WORLD PICTURE
This is mandala, *a Buddhist representation of the world through pictures and diagrams. Buddhists believe that it is possible to overcome suffering in the world if people follow guidelines to help them live a good life.*

AD

c.30 The first Christian churches are founded.

100s Mahayana Buddhism emerges and gradually spreads to China.

313 Christianity is tolerated throughout Roman Empire. Many Romans convert to Christianity.

Jesus Christ

570–632 Life of Muhammad, the founder of Islam.

600s Islam spreads throughout Middle East and North Africa.

Muslim shahadah *(statement of faith)*

600s Buddhism spreads to Tibet and Japan.

680 Decisive split between the Sunni and Shi'ah Muslims.

800s Vikings spread their Norse religion throughout northern Europe.

1054 Christianity splits into Roman Catholic and Orthodox Churches.

1469–1539 Life of Guru Nanak, the first Sikh *guru*.

1517 Roman Catholic Church splits as the Reformation gives rise to Protestant churches.

1699 Guru Gobind Singh forms the *Khalsa* (Sikh community).

1830 Joseph Smith translates the *Book of Mormon*.

Modern Rastafarians

1863 The Baha'i religion is founded.

1870s The Jehovah's Witnesses are formed.

1930–74 Emperor Haile Selassie is Black Messiah to Rastafarians.

Israeli flag

1939–45 More than six million Jews are killed during World War II.

1954 L Ron Hubbard founds the Church of Scientology.

1954 Sun Myung Moon founds the Unification Church, or Moonies.

Ancient Egypt

THE ANCIENT EGYPTIANS lived in the rich and fertile valley of the River Nile, which flowed from Central Africa in the south to the Mediterranean Sea in the north. From around 3100BC they built a great civilization along the river banks which lasted for almost 3,000 years. Ancient Egypt was governed by 31 dynasties (families) of kings, who were known as pharaohs. Pharaohs were believed to be gods on Earth.

Throughout their long history, the Egyptians worshipped many gods, each responsible for a different aspect of daily life. Their main god was Ra, the sun god. He was reborn every morning at dawn and travelled across the sky during the day. In the form of the Sun, Ra brought life to Egypt. He made the plants grow and the animals strong. The ancient Egyptians

▲ THE GREAT PYRAMIDS AT GIZA
Some pharaohs were buried in vast tombs called pyramids. About 100,000 people, many of them slaves, toiled for 20 years to build the Great Pyramid at Giza for Pharaoh Khufu. The shape might have been a symbol of the Sun's rays, or a stairway to heaven.

▶ FLOODS OF TEARS
Osiris was the god of farming. After he was killed by his jealous brother, Seth, Osiris became god of the underworld and the afterlife. Egyptians believed that the yearly flooding of the Nile marked the anniversary of Osiris's death when his queen, Isis, wept for him.

AFTER DEATH
The Egyptians believed that a dead person's spirit would always need a home to return to. That is why they took such trouble to embalm (preserve) dead bodies as mummies. The body was treated with special salt so that it would not rot. Then it was wrapped in linen bandages.

◀ MUMMY MASK
Tutankhamun was a pharaoh who died 3,500 years ago. In 1922 his tomb was discovered. The wrapped-up mummy was wearing a solid-gold death mask. The mummy had been placed in a nest of three ornate wooden coffins, inside a stone box called a sarcophagus.

▶ ANUBIS
The god Anubis led the dead person to the underworld. He was also the god responsible for embalming. Anubis was always shown with the head of a jackal, a type of wild dog. As real jackals often lived in cemeteries, the animal had come to be associated with death.

called their pharaohs the Sons of Ra. Pharaohs were said to be immortal, which meant they would never really die. They were buried in vast pyramids and, later, elaborate underground tombs. Special objects and treasures were buried with them, to ensure that they travelled safely to the afterlife.

The Egyptians believed that everything in life was controlled by the gods. They worshipped them in order to keep them happy and gain their protection. People tried to lead good lives so that, after death, they could enter the next world, which they called the Field of Reeds. They thought this was something like a perfect version of Egypt itself. To get there, first they had to pass through the dangerous *Duat* (underworld). Then they were judged by Osiris, god of the afterlife. If they had lived a good life and passed the test, they would

▲ IN THE BALANCE
In order to get into the heavenly kingdom after death, an Egyptian had to pass a test in a place known as the Hall of Two Truths. The person's heart was weighed to see if it was heavy with sin. If their heart was lighter than the Feather of Truth, the dead person had passed the test and was then presented to Osiris, god of the afterlife. If their heart was heavier, a monster called Ammit ate the heart and the person died forever.

live forever in the Field of Reeds.

The Egyptians placed detailed handbooks in their coffins to help them in this quest. These instruction manuals contained spells for the dead person to recite at each stage of the journey through the *Duat*. The most famous of these manuals is the *Book of the Dead*.

◀ CANOPIC JAR
The liver, lungs, intestines and stomach were removed from the body before it was mummified. The organs were dried out, wrapped in linen and stored in containers called canopic jars.

▶ CAT MUMMY
The Egyptians considered cats to be sacred. Some people even took their dead pet cat to the city of Bubastis, where the cat god Bastet was worshipped. There it would be embalmed and buried in a cat-shaped coffin in the cat cemetery.

▲ EYE OF HORUS
Lucky charms called amulets were wrapped in among a mummy's bandages. The eye amulet stood for the eye of the god Horus, son of Osiris and Isis. Horus lost his eye in a fight with his evil uncle Seth, but it was magically restored. The eye amulet symbolized the victory of good over evil, so everything behind it was protected from evil.

Key Dates

- c.3100BC The Egyptian kingdom is founded.

- c.2630BC First pyramid is built with stepped, not straight, sides.

- c.2528BC Great Pyramid built.

- c.2150BC Last pyramids built.

- 1504–1070BC Nearly all pharaohs, from Thutmose I to Ramses XI (and including the boy-king Tutankhamun), are buried in the Valley of the Kings.

- 332BC Egypt is conquered by the Greek ruler Alexander the Great.

- 30BC Egypt becomes part of the Roman Empire.

The Classical World

THE CIVILIZATION of the ancient Greeks began around 1575BC in Mycenae (southern Greece). The Greeks had no word for religion, yet religion affected every aspect of daily life. People believed that 12 major gods lived on Mount Olympus, the highest mountain in Greece. The god Zeus was their ruler. The gods rewarded good people and they intervened regularly in human affairs.

The Iliad, said to be written by the poet Homer around 800BC, tells the story of the historic siege of Troy by the Greeks. This event from real history is explained and presented as a squabble between the gods. In *The Iliad*, the gods used the Greeks and Trojans to fight on their behalf.

In addition to the pantheon (collection) of 12 main gods, the Greeks believed in the existence of thousands of others. Some gods had more than one role. Athena was the goddess of wisdom and a war goddess, as well as the sacred spirit of the olive tree. She was also the patron (protector) of the city of Athens. Aphrodite was the goddess of love and beauty and also the sacred spirit of the myrtle tree.

The Greeks built temples where they could worship their gods. These were erected in the highest part of a city, which was known as the acropolis. People also built shrines in their homes where they could worship

▲ EARTH AND SKY GOD
Zeus was the king of the gods. As ruler of the sky, he brought rain and storms. As ruler of the land, he took charge of morals and justice.

▶ THE DELPHIC ORACLE
Greeks used to visit the Temple of Apollo in Delphi to consult the oracle. This was the voice of the god Apollo, heard through a young priestess, the Pythia.

ROMAN GODS AND BELIEFS
The city of Rome was founded in 753BC. The Roman Empire grew to one of the largest in the world. When they conquered Greece in 146BC, they added the Greek gods to their own. Often, they changed the gods' names into Latin. By the AD300s, however, many Romans had become Christians and the old gods were neglected.

◀ PAN'S PIPES
Pan was originally the Greek god of the countryside, later associated with the Roman god Faunus. He was usually shown as half-man, half-goat. Pan had many lovers, one of whom, Syrinx, escaped him by turning herself into a reed bed. From these reeds, Pan made a set of musical pipes.

◀ MITHRAIC TEMPLE
The Romans adopted the gods of many peoples they had conquered. Mithras was a Persian god of light and truth. There were Mithraic cults across the Roman Empire.

▶ NIKE
The Greek goddess Nike was known as Victoria to the ancient Romans. She was the goddess of victory. She had a devout following among soldiers in the Roman army.

their favourite gods. This might be a shrine to Hestia, goddess of the hearth (fireplace) and family life. Some gods were worshipped in secret by members of mystery cults. Believers went through a special initiation (joining) ceremony. Once they were in, they took part in elaborate rituals. The two most famous cults were those of Demeter, the goddess of farming and harvests, and Dionysus, the god of wine. Throughout the year, the Greeks celebrated their gods at numerous festivals and ceremonies. In Athens, 120 days of the year were dedicated to festivals.

Stories about the gods and their activities had explained the workings of the world. However, Greek philosophers worked out more everyday explanations. The most famous were Socrates (469–399BC), Plato (c.427–347BC) and Aristotle (384–322BC). As their philosophical ideas took hold, religion became less important to the Greeks and their gods became part of myth and legend.

▲ POSEIDON
Poseidon was god of earthquakes and the sea. He was associated with horses and was said to be the father of Pegasus, the winged horse. Greeks believed that Poseidon was the brother of Zeus and Hades. He was often shown carrying a three-pronged spear, called a trident.

▶ KINGDOMS OF THE GODS
Zeus ruled the land and sky, and Poseidon looked after the sea. Their brother, Hades, was god of the underworld. He ruled there with his wife, Persephone.

▼ JUPITER
The main god of the Romans was Jupiter. Like Zeus, he held supreme power over all the other gods, and showed his power through thunder storms and lightning.

▶ APOLLO
The Greek, and later Roman, god Apollo was associated with light, healing, music, poetry and education.

Greco-Roman gods

These Greek gods were adopted, or adapted, by the Romans. Their Roman names are in brackets.

• Aphrodite (Venus) goddess of love
• Apollo (Apollo) god of healing
• Ares (Mars) god of war
• Artemis (Diana) goddess of hunting
• Demeter (Ceres) goddess of grain
• Dionysus (Bacchus) god of wine
• Hades (Pluto) god of the underworld
• Hephaistos (Hephaestus) god of fire
• Hera (Juno) wife of Zeus (Jupiter)
• Hermes (Mercury) messenger god
• Persephone (Proserpina) goddess of death, queen to Hades (Pluto)
• Poseidon (Neptune) god of earthquakes and the sea
• Zeus (Jupiter) supreme god

Northern Europe

THE VIKINGS OF SCANDINAVIA lived in a cold and inhospitable world of long winters and short summers. They had to fight for their survival. Between the AD800s and 1000s they sailed overseas in search of new lands to conquer and settle. They soon earned a reputation as a warlike people.

Norse, or Scandinavian, religion reflected this harsh way of life. Its origins trace back to the earliest Northern European gods of the Bronze Age. The Vikings believed that the universe was made up of nine different worlds. These were connected by the world tree, Yggdrasil, which was often represented as a giant ash. This tree was thought to contain all the people yet to be born. The world inhabited by people was known as Midgard. The home of the gods was Asgard. The chief Norse god, Odin, lived here, along with all the other gods. He was god of both war and wisdom and had many supernatural powers.

◀ IN DEATH
Vikings were buried with the weapons and treasures that they would need for the next life. Viking chiefs were buried or put out to sea in their boats. Some were laid beneath burial mounds. Even the poorest person was buried with a sword or a brooch.

▶ VIKINGS AND CELTS
Vikings and Celts travelled far in search for new lands to settle. They took their religious beliefs with them. The Celts spread out from the Danube valley across Europe. Viking settlements ranged from North America in the far west to Russia in the east.

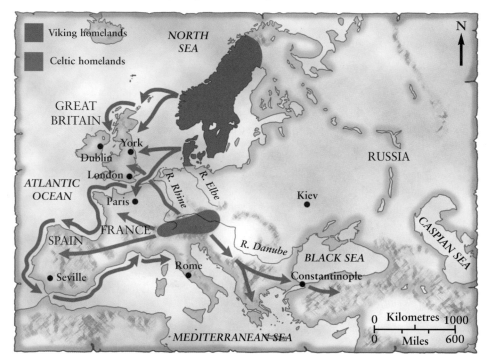

THE CELTS

The Celts spread from their German homeland across the whole of western Europe from around 2000BC. As the Roman Empire expanded, however, the Celts were pushed to the edges of Europe, to Ireland, Scotland, Wales and Brittany. Different, local religions developed, each with its own group of gods. There were common themes, however. The Celts all believed in warrior-heroes with supernatural powers, and they all believed in the sacred Earth Mother. She was the goddess of fertility who brought them life.

▶ MISTLETOE
The druids were the high priests of Celtic religion. They performed the sacred rituals and often used mistletoe in their ceremonies. The plant is still important as part of Christmas festivities.

◀ HARVEST FESTIVAL
From around 2,000 years ago the Celts wove stalks of corn into human 'dollies' or other shapes. These objects were made to give thanks for a successful harvest.

▲ THE LINDISFARNE GOSPEL
The natural world was central to Celtic religion. Celtic influence can be seen in early Christian manuscripts, which were illuminated (illustrated) with pictures of animals and plants.

◀ FREYA
The goddess of love, Freya, was married to Odin, but he left her. Freya wept tears of gold and searched the skies for him in a cat-driven chariot.

▼ RIDE OF THE VALKYRIES
Odin was served by a band of female warriors called the Valkyries. After a battle, Odin and the Valkyries searched the battlefield for dead heroes, whom they carried to Valhalla (Viking heaven).

Vikings believed that the human world, Midgard, was constantly threatened by forces of darkness and evil, such as the frost giants, who covered the world with snow and ice. Thor, the god of thunder, tried to keep these giants away with his hammer. Many Vikings wore a hammer round their necks, or painted a hammer on their door, as protection against evil spirits.

The Vikings held many different beliefs about what happened after death. A sick person who died went to a serpent-filled kingdom ruled by Hel, a witchlike figure. Warriors who died in battle went to Valhalla. This was a huge communal hall, like a perfect version of a Viking longhouse. There were feasting and mock battles there.

By AD1000, many Vikings had become Christians. This is reflected in the late Viking belief that the world would end in one final battle, called the Ragnarok. The gods and forces of evil would destroy themselves in this battle. A new world would be born occupied by two people, Lif and Lifthrasir. Like Adam and Eve, they would worship one supreme god who lived in heaven.

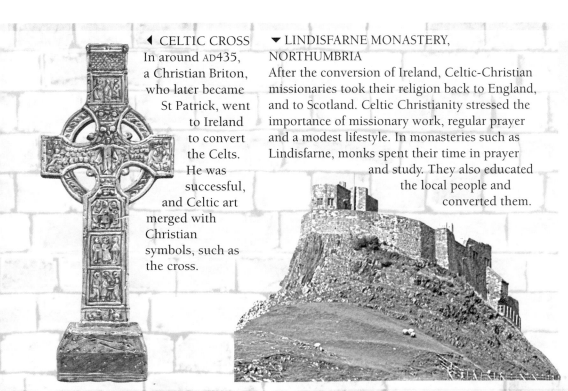

◀ CELTIC CROSS
In around AD435, a Christian Briton, who later became St Patrick, went to Ireland to convert the Celts. He was successful, and Celtic art merged with Christian symbols, such as the cross.

▼ LINDISFARNE MONASTERY, NORTHUMBRIA
After the conversion of Ireland, Celtic-Christian missionaries took their religion back to England, and to Scotland. Celtic Christianity stressed the importance of missionary work, regular prayer and a modest lifestyle. In monasteries such as Lindisfarne, monks spent their time in prayer and study. They also educated the local people and converted them.

Key Dates

- c.2000BC Celtic peoples spread throughout western Europe.
- AD100 The Roman push the Celts to the edges of western Europe.
- c.AD435 St Patrick converts Celts in Ireland to Christianity.
- AD600s Celtic missionaries convert England and Scotland to Christianity.
- AD793 Vikings begin to raid Christian monasteries in Britain.
- AD800s Many Viking raids across northern and western Europe.
- 1000s Vikings begin to convert to Christianity.

Tribal Religions

THE ANCIENT RELIGIONS of Egypt, Greece and Rome disappeared with the fall of the civilizations that fostered them. The same is true of the religions practised by the great peoples of South America, the Mayans, Incas and Aztecs. Other religions, such as those followed by the Vikings and Celts, merged with other beliefs. However, some ancient religions survive to this day, even if they are restricted to one very small area. These are the religions practised by the tribal peoples of Africa, the Americas, Australasia and Asia.

Although these religions vary widely from place to place and people to people, they share much in common. For tribal peoples, the spiritual world plays a very important role in daily life.

The Maasai of East Africa worship a single god, who brings them life from the Sun and makes sure the crops grow. Most tribal peoples, however, believe that there are many gods and spirits. Some spirits are evil and good spirits must be summoned up to overcome them. The Kalabari of eastern Nigeria, for example, make ancestral screens on which they place pictures of their ancestors. Through these, they communicate with the spirit world and try to control the effect that spirits have on their lives. Elsewhere in Africa, local gods protect the oases and waterholes and help to heal the sick.

In all tribal religions, ritual plays an important part in a person's life. Birth, becoming an adult, marriage and death are all celebrated with elaborate ceremonies. Often the

▲ KUBA MASK
Many African peoples, such as the Kuba tribe of Zaire, make sacred masks. These represent the different spirits they call upon at ceremonies to celebrate birth, marriage, or death.

▶ TOTEM POLE
The Native Americans of the Pacific northwest coast carve elaborate totem poles out of tree trunks. Each pole provides a full history of a family. It records the family's earthly history and its relationship with the spirit world. A spirit might take the form of an animal, such as a bear, wolf or eagle.

ABORIGINAL RELIGION
The Aborigines of Australia trace their history back to a time called Dreamtime. This was the time of creation, when ancestral beings shaped the land and made all living things. These beings were half-human and half-animal. Aborigines consider these beings to be their ancestors and also believe that they live on forever as spirits.

◀ HOLY WATER
Aborigines believe that the land is sacred. Mountains, waterholes and other natural features are all places where the spirit world and the natural world combine.

▼ TELLING TALES
Stories of the Dreamtime have been passed down through the generations. One way has been through detailed bark paintings.

◀ ULURU
The ancestral beings created every aspect of the landscape, including Uluru (Ayers Rock). The rock has many sacred caves. It is a special place for all Aborigines.

◀ YANOMAMO SHAMAN
Shamans are healers who contact the spirit world in order to seek divine help. They are common in Siberia and Arctic North America, as well as among the many tribes of South America. These include the Yanomamo peoples who live in the Amazon rainforest, in Brazil.

people wear masks and beautiful costumes. In West Africa, the Mende people hold a masked dance, or masquerade, for young girls when they come of age. This unites all the young women and prepares them for marriage and motherhood. The Dogon of West Africa hold elaborate dances and chant in a secret language when someone dies.

Most common is the worship of ancestors and respect for elderly people in the tribe. This is common in tribes across the world, from the Native Americans to the people of Papua New Guinea. Stories of ancestors' exploits are passed down through the generations. Myths and legends explain how the world was formed and how good and evil came to exist side by side.

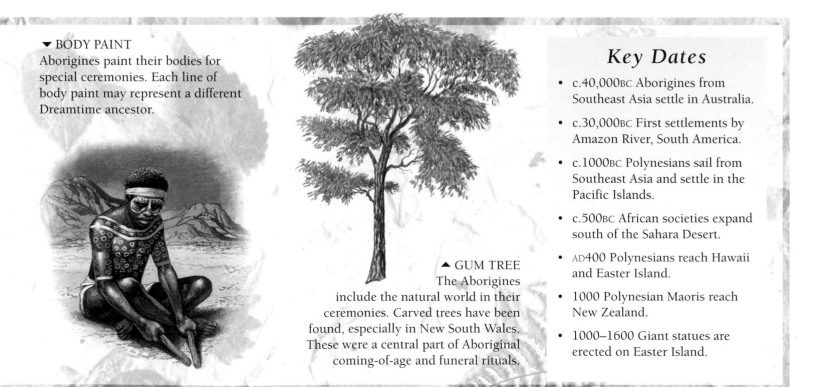

▼ BODY PAINT
Aborigines paint their bodies for special ceremonies. Each line of body paint may represent a different Dreamtime ancestor.

▲ GUM TREE
The Aborigines include the natural world in their ceremonies. Carved trees have been found, especially in New South Wales. These were a central part of Aboriginal coming-of-age and funeral rituals.

Key Dates

- c.40,000BC Aborigines from Southeast Asia settle in Australia.

- c.30,000BC First settlements by Amazon River, South America.

- c.1000BC Polynesians sail from Southeast Asia and settle in the Pacific Islands.

- c.500BC African societies expand south of the Sahara Desert.

- AD400 Polynesians reach Hawaii and Easter Island.

- 1000 Polynesian Maoris reach New Zealand.

- 1000–1600 Giant statues are erected on Easter Island.

Zoroastrianism

THE PROPHET ZOROASTER, OR ZARATHUSTRA as he is also called, was born in northeast Persia (modern-day Iran) around 1200BC. Not much is known about his life, except that he became a priest and was married with several children. His teachings soon became influential. When Cyrus the Great became king of Persia in 539BC, Zoroastrianism became the official religion of his vast empire. In later years, Persian armies spread the religion as far afield as Greece, Egypt and northern India.

For more than 1,000 years, until the arrival of Islam in the AD600s, Zoroastrianism remained a major religion throughout the Middle East. Today it is confined to small pockets in Iran, India – where followers are known as Parsis (Persians) – and East Africa. Zoroastrianism is also practised in a few cities in Europe and North America, but it has fewer than 130,000 believers worldwide.

▲ THE PROPHET
Zoroaster lived in Persia about 1200BC, more than 600 years before the Buddha and 1,200 years before Christ. This makes him the earliest prophet of any world religion.

▶ COMING OF AGE
Young Zoroastrians are welcomed into the faith when they are seven at a special ceremony called the Navjote. *The child is given two sacred objects, a white tunic and a length of cord. The cord, called the* kusti, *has 72 strands of thread. The way the strands join together to work as one has made the* kusti *a symbol of fellowship.*

THE THANKSGIVING CEREMONY
The Zoroastrian ceremony of Jashan (thanksgiving) is to ensure the harmony and well-being of both the spiritual and physical worlds. Zoroastrians offer thanks for their physical lives and ask for blessings from the spiritual world. The Amesha Spentas (spirit guardians of the seven good creations) and the spirits of good people who have died are all invited down to join the ceremony.

◀ AT THE CEREMONY
Jashan is presided over by a *zaotor*, the officiating priest, and a *raspi*, his assistant. Other priests may also be present.

▲ SEVEN GOOD CREATIONS
Everything at Jashan represents one of the seven good creations. A metal cup or tray represents the sky. Fruit represents plants and milk represents cattle. Wine represents humans. Burning sandalwood and frankincense represent the earth. Water and fire represent themselves. Seven flowerbuds represent the Amesha Spentas.

Zoroaster believed that the Supreme God, whom he called Ahura Mazda, had taught him through a series of visions. He learned that there are seven good creations – sky, water, earth, plants, cattle, humans and fire. Each of these is guarded by a spirit. The seven spirit guardians are known as the Amesha Spentas.

Zoroaster wrote his teachings down in 17 *gathas* (hymns) as part of the Zoroastrian sacred scripture, the *Avesta*. The *gathas* are very difficult to read and can be interpreted in many different ways.

According to Zoroaster, the world is a good place, although it contains evil. People can follow Ahura Mazda and live a good life, or they can choose to follow Angra Mainyu, the force of evil. These opposing forces are in constant conflict, but it is everyone's duty to follow good. If they do, they will be rewarded in the afterlife with happiness. If they follow evil, they will only find sorrow.

Zoroaster's teachings have been very influential, even if not many people practise his religion today. Its central ideas of the battle between good and evil and a final day of judgement had a large impact on Judaism, Christianity and Islam.

◀ GUARDIAN SPIRIT
Zoroastrians believe that everyone is looked over by a fravashi, *or guardian spirit. These spirits represent the good in people and help those that ask. The* fravashi *symbol can also represent a person's spiritual self or Ahura Mazda.*

▼ THE TOWER OF SILENCE
Zoroastrians believe that dead bodies provide a home for Angra Mainyu, the force of evil. Bodies cannot be buried in land or sea, nor can they be cremated, since earth, water and fire are all good creations. For this reason, they are left on top of a specially-built tower, the Dakhma (Tower of Silence), as a meal for the vultures.

▲ HOLY SMOKE
Fire is important to Zoroastrians. For them, it is the living symbol of Ahura Mazda. They worship in fire temples and offer prayers to the sacred fire.

▲ ASH SPOT
Before entering a fire temple, Zoroastrians remove their shoes. Once inside, they place a pinch of ash from the sacred fire on their forehead. Then they pray to the fire.

Key Dates

- c.1200BC Birth of Zoroaster.

- 539–331BC Zoroastrianism is the official religion of the Persian Empire.

- 331BC Alexander the Great destroys the Persian Empire and the manuscript of the *Avesta*.

- 129BC Zoroastrianism is again the official religion in Persia.

- c.AD400 The *Avesta* is rewritten.

- AD637 Islam becomes the main religion in Persia.

- AD716 Zoroastrians settle in Gujarat, India. These are the ancestors of modern-day Parsis.

Hinduism

▲ OHM
Every Hindu prayer that is said or sung includes the sound 'Ohm.' The part that looks like a '3' stands for the gods of creation, preservation and death. The part that looks like an 'O' is the silence of god.

THE WORD HINDU comes from the Persian word *sindhu*, which means 'river.' It refers to the religion of the people who lived by the River Indus around 2500BC. This ancient civilization was centred around the cities of Mohenjo-Daro and Harappa (in modern-day Pakistan). Over the centuries, the religion spread across northern India to the valley of the Ganges River.

In the 900s BC, the Hindu scriptures were written down. Two thousand years later Indian rulers took Hinduism to Sri Lanka and Southeast Asia. Today, it is practised around the world. There are more than 800 million Hindus, 700 million of whom live in India.

Hinduism does not have one central belief. It has evolved slowly over time, drawing in ideas from other religions. There are many different types of Hinduism and many different ways to be a Hindu.

Most Hindus believe that they have four aims in life. The first, *dharma*, is to live a good life by being kind to others and telling the truth. The second, *artha*, is to be wealthy and prosperous in life. *Kama* is to enjoy pleasure and *mosksha* is to be freed from the world and its desires.

Hindus also believe that they pass through four stages in life. These are being a student, then a householder, then a thinker and finally an ascetic (someone who is rid of all worldly pleasures). Not everyone achieves these four aims and stages, but if they do, they will be reincarnated (reborn) into a better life. For Hindus, this eternal cycle of life, death and then rebirth into a new life is very important.

◄ BRIDE AND GROOM
A Hindu marriage ceremony contains many religious rituals. At the end of the ceremony, the couple take seven steps, making a vow at each one. The steps represent food, strength, prosperity, well-being, children, happiness and harmony.

HINDU WORSHIP

Worship is an important part of Hindu religion. Hindus worship in temples, at shrines and in their own homes. Most people pray alone, rather than in large groups. Sunrise and sunset are the most popular times of day. Worship can involve singing, prayer and offering up gifts to the gods.

▶ HINDU TEMPLE
Temples have tall, ornate towers and four gateways that represent the four directions of the universe. Hindus visit the temple throughout the day to worship at its main icon (holy image).

◄ SITE OF LIGHT
Varanasi, on the banks of the Ganges, is the most important pilgrimage city in India. Varanasi is known as the City of Light, because it was here that the god Shiva's light reached up to the heavens.

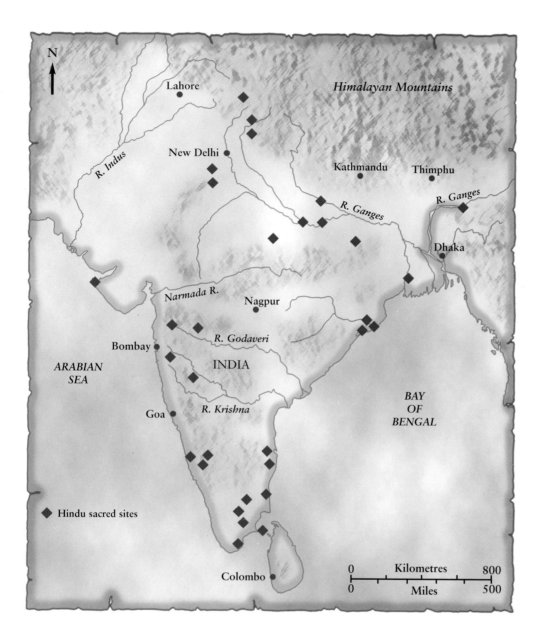

N

Lahore

Himalayan Mountains

R. Indus

New Delhi

Kathmandu

Thimphu

R. Ganges

R. Ganges

Dhaka

Narmada R.

Nagpur

R. Godaveri

Bombay

INDIA

ARABIAN
SEA

R. Krishna

Goa

BAY
OF
BENGAL

◆ Hindu sacred sites

Kilometres
0   800
0   500
Miles

Colombo

◀ THE BIRTH OF HINDUISM

*Hinduism began in the Indus valley
in present-day Pakistan. It spread
throughout northern India, along the
valley of the Ganges. In the early
AD700s, Arab conquerors brought
Islam to the valley of the Indus River.
Over the next seven centuries, Islam
spread slowly across northern India
and sometimes there was conflict
between Hindus and Muslims.*

▼ HINDU PRIESTS

*A brahmin (priest) looks after the
temple and acts as a go-between
between the worshipper and a god.
Wandering priests or holy men are
known as sadhus. These men lead an
ascetic way of life. This means they
give up worldly pleasures and wander
from place to place begging for food.*

▼ PILGRIMAGE
Going on a pilgrimage is an
important part of Hindu worship.
Places of pilgrimage include large
cities, such as Varanasi and sacred
rivers, such as the Ganges. Holy
mountains, temples and small, local
shrines are visited by pilgrims too.

▲ MEMENTO
To remind them of their
pilgrimage, Hindu pilgrims
often bring back small
mementoes from the
shrine they have visited.

Key Dates

- c.1500BC Hindu beliefs spread
  throughout northern India.

- c.900BC Hindu beliefs are
  written down in the four *Vedas*.

- c.500BC The *Mahabharata* written
  down by Vyasa, a wise man.

- c.300BC The *Ramayana* is
  written down by Valmiki, a poet.

- AD850–1200 Chola dynasty of
  northern India takes Hinduism
  to Sri Lanka and Southeast Asia.

- 1900s Hinduism spreads
  throughout world as Indians
  settle in Europe, Africa and the
  Americas.

Hindu Gods and Goddesses

HINDUS BELIEVE IN ONE SUPREME, ultimate god, Brahman, an unseen but all-powerful force who can appear in numerous forms. Some of these forms are worshipped by all Hindus, while others are worshipped only in one place or by a few people. The most important gods are those who created the world and its life and who are powerful enough to destroy it. There are gods of fire and war and many lesser gods that represent the forces of the natural world, such as the Sun and the wind.

Brahman brought the entire universe into existence. However, he is impersonal and takes no recognized appearance for his worshipers. Hindus therefore think of him in a variety of different appearances and worship him that way. The most important way in which Brahman makes himself known is through the Trimurti, a holy trio of three great gods. These are Brahma, Vishnu and Shiva. According to Hindu belief Brahma created the world, Vishnu preserves life and Shiva both destroys life and then recreates it.

Brahma is not worshipped like other gods, because after he created the world he had finished his work. However, when the world ends and needs to be recreated, he will return to create the world all over again. At that time he will be worshipped again.

Vishnu is known as the one who takes many different forms. He is very important because he preserves human life, the life of the world and the life of the universe itself. As a result, his different images are found in many temples and shrines.

▲ DANCE OF DESTRUCTION
Shiva is the destroyer and recreator of life. He is sometimes called the lord of the dance. He ends the dance of life so that a new dance can begin.

▼ BRAHMA
Brahma is the god of creation. After he created the first woman, he fell in love with her, but she hid herself from him. So Brahma grew three more heads so that he could see her from every angle.

GODS IN MANY FORMS

Hindus worship many minor gods. Some, such as Surya the sun god, Indra the god of war, and Vayu the wind god, are described in the Hindu scriptures. Others are specific to particular places. Hindus believe every part of Brahma's creation is divine and worship some animals, including Naga the snake god.

◀ THE ELEPHANT GOD
Ganesh is the remover of obstacles and also the lord of learning. His parents were Shiva and Parvati. One day Ganesh was protecting Parvati but his father did not recognise him and beheaded him. When he realised his mistake, Shiva replaced Ganesh's head with one from the first creature he saw, which was an elephant.

▲ LUCKY LAKSHMI
Lakshmi is one of the many friendly forms of the mother goddess. She is the goddess of fortune and brings wealth and good luck to her followers.

▼ MAHADEVI AS DURGA
Mahadevi is the Hindu mother goddess. She appears in many forms, both fiercesome and gentle. In one form she is the wife of Shiva. As Durga she is a fierce, demon-fighting warrior.

The third god of the trio is Shiva. Like Vishnu, he has many different forms and he has over a thousand names, such as Maheshvara, the lord of knowledge, and Mahakala, the lord of time. He is often shown with three faces. Two of the faces have opposite characteristics, such as male and female, or peace and war. The third face is always calm, to reconcile (bring together) the two opposites.

▶ RESTORING HARMONY
Vishnu is the god who preserves life, maintaining the balance between good and evil in the universe. If evil seems about to take control, Vishnu comes down to Earth to restore the balance. On Earth Vishnu takes the form of one of his ten incarnations, or avatars, the most important being Krishna. Nine of these avatars have visited the Earth already. The final one will arrive when the Earth is nearing the end of its current life. This tenth incarnation of Vishnu will destroy the world, then recreate it.

Kurma, the turtle

Matsya, the fish

Varaha, the boar

Narasimha, half-man, half-goat

Vamana, the dwarf

Rama

Krishna

Krishna with his mistress, Radha

Parasurama

Buddha

Kalki

▲ MONKEY GOD
The epic poem the *Ramayana* tells how the monkey god, Hanuman, helped Rama to defeat the demon king Ravana. Hanuman is worshipped as the god of strength and heroism.

▼ KARTTIKEYA
The boy god Karttikeya has many different names and there are many different stories about who his parents were. He was born to defeat evil and is often shown with a peacock, which is the national bird of India.

Ten Avatars of Vishnu

1. Matsya the fish, who saved the law-giver Manu during the Flood.
2. Kurma the turtle, who held the Earth on his back after the Flood.
3. Varaha the boar, who raised the land out of the water with his tusks.
4. Narasimha, who destroyed the demon king, Hiranyakasipu.
5. Vamana the dwarf, who tricked Hiranyakasipu's evil nephew, Bali.
6. Parasurama, who defeated an army of warriors with his axe.
7. Rama, who killed King Ravana.
8. Krishna, who told the *Bhagavad Gita* to Arjuna, his chariot driver.
9. Buddha, who founded Buddhism.
10. Kalki, who will appear at the end of the world on a white horse.

Hindu Scriptures

▲ A YOGI
Yogis are holy men who practise yoga, which means union of the individual soul with the universe. Yogis have played an important part in bringing Hindu teachings and scriptures to a wide audience in Europe and the Americas.

THE HINDU RELIGIOUS BOOKS were written down in Sanskrit (the ancient language of India) over the course of more than 1,000 years. Hindus have many different types of scripture, which fall into three groups.

The first group, the four *Vedas*, were originally passed down by word of mouth from generation to generation. *Veda* means 'knowledge.' The *Rig Veda* was the first to be written down in about 1200BC. It contains religious hymns. Next came the *Sama Veda*, which consists of chants for Hindus to sing as part of their worship, and the *Yajur Veda*, which contains words to be spoken by Hindu priests. The last one was written in about 900BC. This is the *Atharva Veda*, which is full of magic spells and incantations. Hindus believe the words of the *Vedas* are divine, so not a single word of them can be changed.

▲ THE VEDAS
The four Vedas *are the oldest Hindu scriptures of all. The oldest and best known, the* Rig Veda, *contains holy songs about the ancient gods of fire, earth, air and water. These were written to be accompanied by traditional Indian instruments, such as the sitar, shenai (a reed instrument) and the tabla (a type of drum).*

From around 700BC, Hindus began to wonder about the meaning of life and other philosophical questions. Over the next 400 years, this gave rise to the second major group of religious books. The *Upanishads* (sittings near a teacher) answer such questions as where we come from and why are we here. They explore the key concepts of Hinduism, such as reincarnation. They describe ordinary life as a cycle of birth, suffering, death and rebirth, and urge people to seek *moksha* (freedom from cycle of death and rebirth). The *Aranyakas* (forest books) deal with the meaning of rituals. The *Puranas* (ancient myths) contain stories of creation and the lives of the

FESTIVALS AND CELEBRATIONS
The Hindu year is filled with many festivals celebrating the gods and natural events, such as the end of winter or the rice harvest. Some are national festivals celebrated by Hindus all over the world. Others are celebrated only in particular parts of India.

◄ THE FESTIVAL OF LIGHTS
The five-day festival of Diwali celebrates the return of the god Rama from exile. Diwali is held in October or November. Candles are lit in every house so as to welcome Lakshmi, goddess of wealth.

▲ SPRING CELEBRATIONS
Holi, celebrated in March, marks the start of spring and the Hindu New Year. Holi is a fun festival. People of all castes (classes) join in by throwing coloured powders over each other.

▼ EFFIGIES FOR BURNING
Dusserah lasts nine days and is a celebration of good winning over evil. In southern India people burn effigies (models) of demons to symbolize Rama's victory over the evil king, Ravana.

gods. As in the *Vedas*, the words in the *Upanishads* are holy and cannot be changed.

The final group of religious books are two epic poems. The first of these appeared in about 500BC. The *Mahabharata* is the longest poem in the world, with more than 200,000 lines. It includes myths and philosophical discussions. At the heart of the book is the *Bhagavad Gita* (Song of the Lord), which is a conversation between Krishna, one of the avatars of Vishnu, and his chariot driver, Arjuna. The second epic, the *Ramayana*, was written down in about 300BC. It tells the story of Rama, another avatar of Vishnu, and how he rescued his wife, Sita, who had been kidnapped by the demon king, Ravana, king of Lanka.

▲ AN ILLUSTRATION FROM THE MAHABHARATA
Much of the Mahabharata *concerns a long war between two families, the Kauravas and the Pandavas. Along the way there are many tales that explain aspects of history. One tells how the River Ganges came to be. Another describes the Great Flood.*

▲ SITA IN RAVANA'S PALACE
The Ramayana *(Rama's Progress) was a popular folk story long before it was written down. In it, the evil king Ravana captures Rama's wife, Sita. He carries her off to his palace in Lanka (modern-day Sri Lanka). It was years before Rama rescued her.*

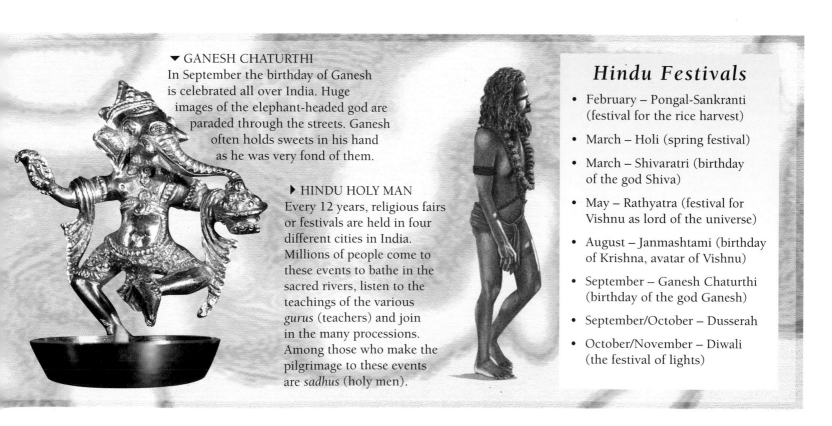

▼ GANESH CHATURTHI
In September the birthday of Ganesh is celebrated all over India. Huge images of the elephant-headed god are paraded through the streets. Ganesh often holds sweets in his hand as he was very fond of them.

▶ HINDU HOLY MAN
Every 12 years, religious fairs or festivals are held in four different cities in India. Millions of people come to these events to bathe in the sacred rivers, listen to the teachings of the various *gurus* (teachers) and join in the many processions. Among those who make the pilgrimage to these events are *sadhus* (holy men).

Hindu Festivals

- February – Pongal-Sankranti (festival for the rice harvest)
- March – Holi (spring festival)
- March – Shivaratri (birthday of the god Shiva)
- May – Rathyatra (festival for Vishnu as lord of the universe)
- August – Janmashtami (birthday of Krishna, avatar of Vishnu)
- September – Ganesh Chaturthi (birthday of the god Ganesh)
- September/October – Dusserah
- October/November – Diwali (the festival of lights)

Jainism

▲ PALM OF PEACE
The open palm is the official symbol of Jainism. It represents peace. Sometimes the word Ahimsa *(non-violence) is written on the palm.*

THE JAIN RELIGION began in the valley of the Ganges River, India, in around 500BC. It slowly spread throughout northern India and today has 4.5 million followers in India, mainly in the business community. It also flourishes in Indian communities elsewhere in the world, such as in the USA.

Jainism was founded by a rich man, Mahavira. At the age of 29 he renounced (gave up) his wealth and became an ascetic, giving up worldy goods and begging for his food. He wanted to break the endless cycle of birth, life, death and rebirth, by finding enlightenment, or spiritual peace. After 12 years of fasting and meditation, he achieved *kevala* (perfect knowledge). He then assembled a group of 12 followers and spent the next 30 years as a preacher until he starved to death at Pava, a village not far from his birthplace. Today Pava is one of the holiest sites of the Jain religion.

Jains take their name from *jina*. A *jina* is someone who has reached enlightenment. Jains believe that time is endless and is divided into a series of upward or downward movements that can last millions of years. In each of these movements, 24 *jinas* appear. Mahavira was the most recent. The *jinas* come to guide others towards enlightenment. They are also called *tirthankaras*.

Jains study the teachings of the *tirthankaras* and also take five vows to help them achieve spiritual peace. The vows are *ahimsa* (not to harm any living thing), *satya* (to speak the truth), *asteya* (not to steal), *brahmacharya* (to abstain from sexual activity) and *aparigraha* (not to become attached to people, places or possessions).

▼ RESPECT FOR LIFE
Monks and nuns often wear masks to stop them breathing in and killing insects. They also carry a brush to sweep insects out of the way so that they do not tread on them.

JAIN BELIEFS
Jains do not believe in a god and they do not pray to gods to help them in their lives. Instead, they study the works of the *tirthankaras* and practise meditation and self-discipline. They believe this is their only hope of release from the world and achieving spiritual liberation. Many Jains have jobs and live in the material world. Some Jains become monks or nuns to keep their mind uncluttered as they search for enlightenment.

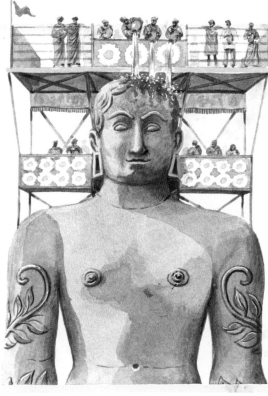

◀ LORD BAHUBALI
Bahubali defeated his half-brother in battle but did not kill him. Instead, he became a holy man. Jains consider him to be the first *tirthankara* of the present age. Every 12 years, pilgrims go to the Indian town of Sravanabegola to worship at his giant statue and anoint it with coloured water.

▲ PARSHVANATHA, 23RD TIRTHANKARA
The word tirthankara means 'builder of the ford.' Jains believe that they help people across samsara (the river of rebirth) to spiritual freedom. This page shows the 23rd Tirthankara.

Although there are not many Jains in the world today, their belief in non-violence has had a major effect on modern politics. The Indian leader Mahatma Gandhi, who led his country to independence from Britain in 1947, was profoundly influenced by the idea of non-violence, although he was not a Jain himself. Gandhi used it as a political weapon. Through his example, non-violent protest has become common in modern times, especially in the USA, where Martin Luther King and the Civil Rights movement achieved change peacefully in the 1960s.

▼ PLACE OF WORSHIP
A Jain temple is elaborately constructed, with many courtyards, balconies, domes and spires. At its centre is a shrine that contains a sacred image of one of the tirthankaras. *Worshippers meditate quietly or chant a* mantra *(prayer).*

▼ PICTURING THE UNIVERSE
The Jains see the universe, or *loka*, as divided into three main sections. At the bottom are eight hells and at the top are many heavens. In between is the *Madhya Loka* (middle world), which contains rings of continents and oceans. In the centre of these rings is the *Jambudvipa*, where Jains live.

▶ HEAVEN ON EARTH
Jain temples are meant to be earthly replicas of the *samasavarana* (the heavenly halls where the *tirthankaras* live). That is why Jain temples are so beautiful.

Key Dates

- c. 800BC Parsva, the last-but-one *tirthankara*, lives in India.
- c. 500BC Mahavira, the last *tirthankara*, founds Jainism, which spreads throughout northern India.
- c.AD300 Jainism splits into two groups, the Digambaras and Shvetambaras. They have different ideas about the status of women and how detached from daily life a Jain should be.
- AD981 Giant statue of Bahubali is built at Sravanabegola.
- 1900s The idea of non-violence influences political protests.

Buddhism

▲ THE EIGHTFOLD PATH
An eight-spoked wheel is the symbol for the Noble Eightfold Path. These eight different states of mind sum up the Buddha's teaching on how to find enlightenment.

BUDDHISM WAS founded by Siddhartha Gautama, who became known as the Buddha (enlightened one). The Buddha was born in northern India in 485BC. By the time of his death in 405BC, his teachings had spread across India, eventually reaching Southeast Asia, Korea and Japan. Today, there are more than 330 million Buddhists around the world, mainly in eastern Asia but also in Europe and North America.

The Buddha taught that it was possible to overcome suffering in the world and become enlightened by following the Eightfold Path. The steps along this path are right knowledge, right attitude, right speech, right actions, right livelihood, right effort, right state of mind and right concentration. Buddhists must make sure that each of these aspects of their life is *samma* (right). The Eightfold Path involves a great deal of discipline, so Buddhists often find a teacher to help

them. Once they have understood the path, they try to practise it. This takes them towards enlightenment and, ultimately, they aim for *nirvana* (a state of supreme happiness and bliss).

Nirvana is difficult to achieve, for Buddhists believe that we constantly travel through an endless cycle of life, death and rebirth, either as humans or in other forms. All these lives are subject to *karma* (the law of cause and effect). This means that every action has a result, either good or bad. If we do bad things, we increase our negative *karma* and keep being reborn into new lives. If we do good things, we gain positive *karma*.

Buddhists try to get rid of negative *karma* by

◄ BUDDHA'S FOOTPRINT
The Buddha did not want his followers to make him into a god, so at first there were no statues of him. He was shown only through symbols, such as his footprint.

THE SPREAD OF BUDDHISM
Buddhism began in northern India in around 500BC and then spread to Sri Lanka, Southeast Asia and into Tibet, China and Japan. The early forms of Buddhism are known as Theravada (teaching of the elders). In the first century AD, a new branch of Buddhism developed called Mahayana (great vehicle).

▶ BUDDHISM DIVIDED
Theravada Buddhism is strongest in Sri Lanka and Southeast Asia. Mahayana Buddhism is practised in Tibet, Mongolia, China, Korea, Japan and Vietnam.

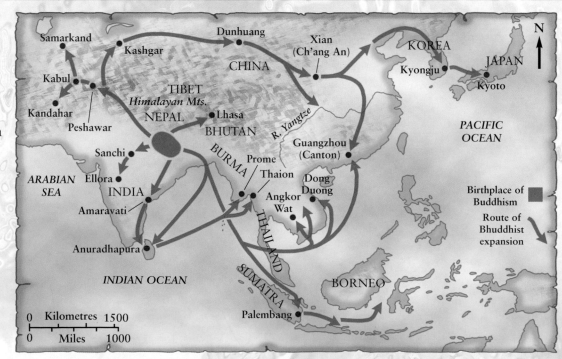

▼ HUMAN FAILINGS
At the centre of the Wheel of Life are three animals. They symbolize the weaknesses that human beings must overcome. The pig represents greed. The cockerel stands for delusion (holding false beliefs). The last creature, the snake, symbolizes hatred.

following the Eightfold Path, doing good deeds and by meditating. They believe that if they succeed, they will be released from the law of *karma* and stop *samsara* (wandering from life to life). They will be free from suffering and achieve the peace of *nirvana*.

The Buddha preached that life is always changing and that people should not look for happiness in material things, such as wealth and possessions. Instead, they should get rid of fear, passion, greed, ignorance, selfishness, and all the other vices that keep them attached to the world. In this way, they become enlightened and can achieve *nirvana*.

▲ THE WHEEL OF LIFE
Buddhists believe that when a person dies, they are reborn into one of six realms (regions) of existence. The gods, the fighting gods, the hungry ghosts, hell, beasts and humans each have their own realm, shown on this thangka, *or religious drawing.*

◀ BUDDHIST MONK
The Buddha formed his own community of monks, the *Sangha*. Monks are an important part of Buddhism to this day. They teach people how to achieve *nirvana*, in return for food and clothes.

▶ BODHISATTVA
A person who has achieved enlightenment but decides to stay in the world to help others is known as a *bodhisattva* (one who is possessed of enlightenment).

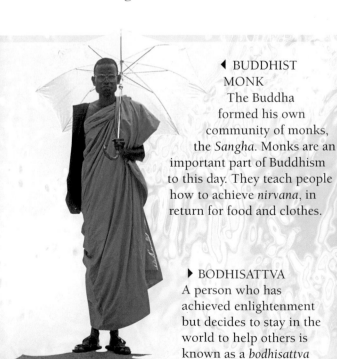

Key Dates

- 485–405BC Life of the Buddha.
- 250BC Buddhism spreads to Sri Lanka and Southeast Asia.
- AD100s Mahayana Buddhism emerges.
- AD100s Buddhism spreads to China and Central Asia.
- AD300s Buddhism reaches Korea.
- AD600s Buddhism reaches Tibet and Japan.
- AD868 The sacred Buddhist text, the *Diamond Sutra*, is printed.
- 1000s Buddhism dies out in India as Muslim armies invade.

The Life of the Buddha

▲ LOTUS FLOWER
The waterlily or lotus flower often symbolizes Buddhism. The flower stands for enlightenment, because it grows out of slimy mud, which symbolizes suffering.

PRINCE SIDDHARTHA Gautama was born into a royal family in northeastern India in 485BC. His father sheltered him from the suffering in the world, but while he was out of the palace one day Gautama came face to face with a sick man, then an old man and finally a dead man. He was only 29, but Gautama understood that sickness, old age and death would come to him eventually, too. He decided to follow a holy, way of life in order to come to terms with the meaning of life. He left behind his wife and family and lived a poor life without any luxuries at all. He meditated every day and fasted (did not eat). Gautama suffered a great deal. His hair fell out and he grew thin and weak. After six

years, Gautama decided that his extreme lifestyle was not the best way to find peace. He decided to find a middle way, somewhere between an ascetic, monk-like existence and a life in the everyday world.

One evening, Gautama was sitting in the shade of a bodhi tree (tree of enlightenment) in Bodh Gaya, a village in northeastern India. After meditating here for a long time, he achieved the state of perfect peace, or *nirvana*. From this moment on, he became known as the Buddha (enlightened one). Today the sacred Mahabodhi temple stands on the site of Buddha's enlightenment.

During his deep meditation the Buddha came to understand the Four Noble Truths. These are the central Buddhist teachings. By understanding these truths, and following the Eightfold Path of right living,

◄ GOLDEN BUDDHA
From around 200BC, people began to build statues of the Buddha. He is usually shown sitting cross-legged, with each foot resting on the opposite thigh. This is called the lotus position. It is used in yoga to help concentrate the mind.

BUDDHIST TEMPLES

When the Buddha died, his remains were divided and *stupas* (Buddhist burial mounds) were built over them. These soon became places of pilgrimage and were often decorated with elaborate carvings and encrusted with stone. Shrines and temples to the Buddha or *bodhisattvas* are found throughout the Buddhist world.

▶ KATHESIMBHU
Buddhists make pilgrimages to this stupa in Nepal to see relics of the Buddha.

◄ BOROBUDUR
The Buddhist temple at Borobudur on the Indonesian island of Java has a central stupa at the top. It is reached by climbing past eight terraces, shaped as squares and circles. These represent a Buddhist's journey from hell, through earthly life and up to heavenly worlds at the summit.

a person can rise above suffering and achieve the state of *nirvana*.

The Buddha gathered together a group of five disciples (followers) and took up a life as a holy teacher. For the next 45 years he travelled around northern India, teaching his message and begging for food. His first sermon was at Sarnath, near Varanasi in northeast India. He preached in a deer park, which is why some images of the Buddha show him with deer at his feet.

When the Buddha died, his last words to his followers were, "Do not cry. Have I not told you that it is in the nature of all things, however dear they may be to us, that we must part with them and leave them." He meant that Buddhists must not be too attached to anything, as this will only bring sorrow and suffering and will hinder them on their quest for *nirvana*.

◀ DEATH OF THE BUDDHA
When the Buddha died at the age of 80, he became known as the Tathagata (Thus-gone). Having achieved nirvana when he died, the Buddha was not reborn into life again like other people. Buddhists believe he moved beyond life to a blissful state where he neither existed nor did not exist.

▶ TEMPLE
At the centre of a Buddhist temple is a shrine that houses images of Buddha and other holy men. Leading off from it are rooms for meditation and teaching.

▼ MONASTERY
Buddhists as young as eight years old enter monasteries, where they study to become monks. Monasteries usually have classrooms, libraries, rooms for meditation and shrines.

▼ TRAVELLING TEMPLE
In Thailand, tiny temples containing a statue of the Buddha are carried to remote parts. This gives villagers a place to worship.

The Four Noble Truths

The Buddha revealed these Four Truths in his first sermon at Sarnath. They form the basis of all his other teachings. To understand them you must concentrate, and be peaceful.

1. Suffering exists in the world and so all existence is *dukka* (full of suffering and dissatisfaction).

2. Suffering exists because of *tamba* (the yearning for satisfaction).

3. The only way to overcome suffering is to achieve *nirvana*.

4. *Nirvana* can be reached by following the Eightfold Path.

Types of Buddhism

As Buddhism spread from India throughout the rest of Eastern Asia, it changed. It adapted to local cultures and adopted elements from other religions. Early Buddhism emphasized the importance of meditation. It stressed that people are on their own in the world and can reach *nirvana* only through their own efforts. This strand of Buddhism is known as Theravada (the teaching of the elders). The other strand of Buddhism is known as Mahayana (great vehicle). Followers of Mahayana believe that people are not alone and that they must work together to achieve *nirvana*. Help also comes from the Buddha, other *buddhas* (enlightened ones) and

▲ PRAYER WHEEL
Tibetan Buddhists often carry a prayer wheel with a mantra *(chant) inside on a strip of paper. Each turn of the wheel counts as a single prayer.*

▶ WORLD PICTURE
A mandala is a representation of the world through pictures and diagrams. It can be a vast temple, or a picture printed on paper or silk. Tantric Buddhists chant mantras over mandalas as they are made. They believe that they give off powerful energy.

BUDDHISM ABROAD

Buddhism varies from country to country, but two aspects of the religion are common to Buddhists everywhere. Monks are important, especially to Tibetan Buddhists. Meditation is practised by all Buddhists, but especially by the Zen Buddhists of Japan. When they meditate, Buddhists rid their minds of all thoughts and find inner stillness. In this state, they can concentrate on gaining enlightenment.

◀ THE DALAI LAMA
The leader of Tibet is the Dalai Lama. The present Dalai Lama left Tibet in 1959, eight years after China first occupied his country. From his exile in India, he has campaigned peacefully for China to restore Tibet's independence.

▲ HEADDRESS
Some Tibetan *lamas* wear headdresses for religious services. This one shows the five *buddhas* of meditation.

◀ SPIRITUAL HOME
The Potala stands high on a hilltop in Lhasa, the Tibetan capital. It is the traditional palace of the Dalai Lama, though the present Dalai Lama is in exile. It also serves as a temple and monastery and houses the tombs of previous Dalai Lamas.

bodhisattvas. Bodhisattvas are people who have already reached *nirvana*, but have chosen to stay in the world to help others achieve it too. Both Theravada and Mahayana Buddhists believe that the Buddha himself was only one in a long line of enlightened people, and that many other *buddhas* exist as well.

Mahayana Buddhism differs from country to country. In China, Buddhism was practised alongside the ancient Chinese religions of Confucianism and Taoism. Many *bodhisattvas* acquired Chinese names. In Tibet, the use of ritual, symbolism, meditation and magic became important. Tantric Buddhism, as it is known, uses mantras or sacred chants written in *tantras* (secret books) to help people attain *nirvana*. Spiritual teachers, known as *lamas*, educate people in Buddhism. *Lamas* are also said to guide a dying person's spirit between death and rebirth.

In Japan, Zen Buddhism adapted the Chinese practice of meditation. Zen meditation requires the person to sit cross-legged in the lotus position. As they meditate, they think about a *koan* (riddle), such as 'What is the sound of one hand clapping?'. The purpose behind such riddles is to make people focus on the meanings behind words. In this way, they escape their conventional ways of thinking and free their minds to reach *nirvana*. Zen meditation can take place in a garden, a teahouse or even through practising ancient arts, such as flower arranging or archery.

▶ THE BOOK OF BUDDHISM
This picture of the Buddha preaching is based on an illustration in the Diamond Sutra. *This sacred Buddhist scroll is five metres long and contains one of the Buddha's sermons. It is the world's oldest printed book.*

◀ JAPANESE TEAHOUSE
Teahouses are beautiful places to meditate. The *sado* (tea ceremony) was perfected in the 1500s by Sen Rikyu. He stressed the importance of *wabi* (simplicity) and *sabi* (peacefulness).

▼ ZEN GARDEN
Zen Buddhists create peaceful gardens as places for meditation. Instead of colourful flowers, there are rocks, sand and grass. Raking the sand into patterns can be a form of meditation in itself.

The Buddhist Year

- In India, Buddhist New Year is celebrated in March or April. In Tibet, it is celebrated in February.

- The birth of Buddha, known as Vesakha in Theravada Buddhism, is celebrated in May.

- In Tibet, Buddha's enlightenment is celebrated in May.

- Buddha's Asalha (first sermon) is celebrated by Theravada Buddhists in July.

- Kattika is a Theravada festival to celebrate missionaries who spread the Buddha's teachings. It is held in late November.

Sikhism

▲ THE KHANDA
Every part of the Sikh emblem, the khanda, *has a meaning. The double-edged sword in the centre stands for truth and justice. The ring symbolizes the unity of God. The two curved swords at the bottom stand for spiritual and earthly power.*

THE SIKH RELIGION was founded by Guru Nanak. He was born in the Punjab province of what is now Pakistan and northwestern India in 1469. The Sikh holy book, the *Guru Granth Sahib*, was gathered together by the end of the 1500s. Despite persecution by Hindu and Muslim rulers of India, Sikhism slowly gained strength. Today there are more than 20 million Sikhs, mainly in the Punjab but also wherever Punjabis have settled in the world, notably Britain, East Africa, Malaysia, and North America. The word *sikh* is Punjabi for 'learner.' Sikhs see themselves as learning their faith from one true teacher, Sat Guru (the Sikh god). *Gurus* (teachers) reveal God's teachings. The Sikhs recognize 12 *gurus* in total. They are God, ten leaders of the faith, and the *Guru*

Granth Sahib, the holy book.

The first *guru* was Nanak. He lived during a period of great conflict between Hindus and Muslims in India. Some Hindus were seeking a god above any religious conflict, and Nanak joined them in their search.

"There is no Hindu or Muslim, so whose path shall I follow?" he wondered. Nanak came to believe that there was one God, who created everything, and that everything depended on him. Nanak also believed that God does not appear on Earth but makes himself known through teachers, or *gurus*.

Sikh beliefs are summed up in the words of the *Mool Mantra*, the first hymn written by Guru Nanak.

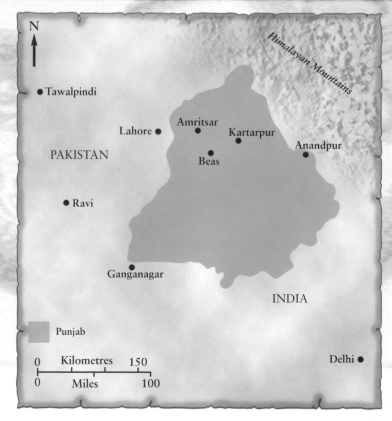

◀ GURU NANAK
The founder of the Sikh religion was born in the Punjab in 1469. Born a Hindu, Nanak did not agree with the religious wars at the time. He also felt that too much ritual made God distant to us.

THE SIKH HOMELAND

Sikhs were often under attack from Muslim, Hindu and Afghan armies so, in 1799, they established their own kingdom in the Punjab. This lasted until British forces occupied it in 1849. When the British left in 1947, the Punjab was split between India and Pakistan. Since the 1980s, some Sikhs have campaigned for the Punjab to become an independent Sikh state. This would be called Khalistan (the land of the *Khalsa*).

N

Himalayan Mountains

• Tawalpindi

Lahore •   Amritsar •   • Kartarpur

PAKISTAN   • Anandpur
          Beas •

• Ravi

Ganganagar •

INDIA

Punjab

| 0 | Kilometres | 150 |
| 0 | Miles | 100 |

Delhi •

▲ GURU RAM DAS
Ram Das became the fourth *guru* in 1574. He founded the city of Amritsar. His followers dug out the Harimandir Sahib, the vast holy lake that surrounds the Golden Temple.

▶ THE GOLDEN TEMPLE
Guru Nanak saw that it was easy for worship to become a meaningless ritual. He said that God can always be found within oneself. However, as long as Sikhs understand that buildings are not holy in themselves, they can build temples at important holy sites. The Golden Temple at Amritsar, Punjab, is the holiest Sikh shrine. It was built in 1601 and contains the Guru Granth Sahib, *the holy book of the Sikhs.*

"There is only God. Truth is his name. He is the creator. He is without fear. He is without hate. He is timeless and without form. He is beyond death, the enlightened one. He can only be known by the Guru's grace." Sikhs meditate so that they can understand the *gurus'* teachings.

Nanak ensured that after his death another *guru* would take over and continue his work. Nanak died in 1539. Nine more *gurus* carried Sikhism forward until the death of Guru Gobind Singh in 1708. Guru Gobind Singh chose the Sikh holy scripture, not a person, to be his successor. That is why the scripture is called the *Guru Granth Sahib* and is considered to be the 11th guru. The holy book and its teachings guide the Sikh community to this day.

▼ GURU ARJAN
Arjan became the fifth *guru* in 1581. He collected all the hymns of previous *gurus* with his own contributions and combined them into the *Guru Granth Sahib*, the Sikh holy book. He died in 1606.

▲ GURU HAR KRISHAN
Har Krishan was only five when he became the eighth *guru* in 1661. He died of smallpox three years later. He is the only *guru* to be shown without a beard, because he was too young to grow one.

▼ GURU GOBIND SINGH
Gobind Singh, the tenth *guru*, is the second-most important *guru* after Guru Nanak. He established the *Khalsa* (community of Sikhs) and resisted the Hindu and Muslim rulers of India.

Key Dates

- 1469–1539 Life of Guru Nanak, the first *guru*.
- 1577 Guru Ram Das founds the city of Amritsar.
- 1604 The *Guru Granth Sahib* is installed in the Golden Temple.
- 1699 Guru Gobind Singh forms the *Khalsa* (Sikh community).
- 1799 Maharajah Ranjit Singh founds an independent Sikh kingdom in the Punjab.
- 1849 The Punjab becomes part of British India.
- 1947 The Punjab is split between India and Pakistan.

Sikh Teachings

IN 1699 THE LAST of the ten *gurus*, Guru Gobind Singh, called the Sikhs together at the *mela* (fair) in Anandpur. He called for a volunteer who was willing to die for his faith. One man stepped forward and went into a tent with the *guru*, who came out soon afterwards with a bloody sword. Four more men then volunteered, and they also followed the guru into the tent. Then the *guru* opened the tent and revealed that all the five men were still alive.

This event marks the start of the *Khalsa* (Sikh community) whose members pledge to uphold the Sikh religion and defend all those in need, perhaps even to lose their lives for their faith. In order to make all Sikhs equal, Guru Gobind Singh gave all men the name Singh (lion) and all women the name Kaur (princess).

▲ THE CHAURI
The chauri, or whisk, is a symbol of authority. Just as a whisk was waved over a guru to keep the flies away in the Punjab, so the chauri is waved over the holy book to show respect for it.

▶ THE GURU GRANTH SAHIB
The Sikh holy book is a collection of teachings by Guru Nanak and other gurus. The book starts with verses written by Nanak, which are recited everyday by Sikhs in their morning prayers.

FESTIVALS
All Sikh festivals are times of meditation and thought. Sikhs hold two types of festival. *Gurpurbs* remember the birth or martyrdom of one of the ten gurus. Sikhs prepare for a *gurpurb* by reading the whole of the *Guru Granth Sahib*, which takes about 48 hours. *Melas* are fairs. They are times of strenuous activity, with sports events, mock battles, and firework displays.

▼ SIKH WEDDINGS
When Sikhs marry, the bride and groom's families are joined together as well. Verses from the *Guru Granth Sahib* are read out, and the couple walk around the holy book after each verse as part of their wedding vows.

▼ GOBIND SINGH'S BIRTHDAY
At the festival to celebrate Guru Gobind Singh's birthday, Sikhs read the *Guru Granth Sahib*, pray, meditate and sing together. People wear traditional costume.

kara

kirpan

kangha

◀ THE FIVE Ks ▶

When the Khalsa *was founded in 1699, Guru Gobind Singh asked Sikhs to wear five symbols to show their allegiance to the Sikh community. These are known as the Five Ks, because their names all begin with the letter 'k.' They are* kirpan *(a curved dagger),* kangha *(a comb),* kara *(a steel bangle),* kachh *(short pants worn as underwear) and* kesh *(uncut hair). Sikh boys and men wear a turban to keep their* kesh *tidy. However, the turban itself is not one of the Five Ks.*

Sikhs become members of the *Khalsa* in an initiation ceremony known as an *amrit sanskar*, which is often performed at the Vaisakhi festival held in April to commemorate the founding of the *Khalsa*. The ceremony is private, and takes place in the local *gurdwara* (Sikh temple). Many Sikhs wait until they are adults before joining the *Khalsa*, although boys as young as 14 do join. Women can join, but it is rare for them to do so. All candidates must be approved by existing members of the *Khalsa*.

At the ceremony, five members of the *Khalsa* each hand over one of the Five Ks to the new recruit. These are symbolic objects that all Sikhs must have. In return, the young Sikh pledges to defend the faith, serve other people, pray every morning and evening, and not to smoke or drink alcohol. He is then given a sweet drink called *amrit* and says that "The *Khalsa* is of God and the victory is to God." After a few prayers, the new recruit is admitted to the *Khalsa*.

Sikh religious and community life revolves around the *gurdwara*. Its name means 'the door of the *guru*.' This is where the *Guru Granth Sahib* is kept, and were Sikhs gather to sing, meditate and study. There is no holy day of the week reserved for worship as in many of the other religions. Services can take place at any time.

▼ HOLY LITTER
The *Guru Granth Sahib* takes pride of place in any festival procession. It is carried on a litter by five Sikh elders, dressed in yellow and white. The litter is decorated with garlands.

▲ ANANDPUR FAIR
At the time of the Hindu festival of Holi, Sikhs gather for a *mela* (fair) to remember the life of Guru Gobind Singh. They hold athletic and horse-riding events and compete in the martial arts. The greatest of these *melas* is the Hola Mohalla in Anandpur, Punjab.

Sikh Festivals

- December/January – Guru Gobind Singh's birthday.
- February – Hola Mohalla, in memory of Guru Gobind Singh.
- April – Formation of the *Khalsa*.
- May – Martyrdom of Guru Arjan (1606).
- August – Celebration of the *Guru Granth Sahib* (1606).
- October – The Hindu festival of Diwali marks Guru Hargobind's release from prison in 1619.
- October – Guru Nanak's birthday.
- November – Martyrdom of Guru Tegh Bahadur (1675).

Religion in China

▲ THE I CHING
The I Ching *is based on the ancient art of divination, telling the future. Special disks might be thrown. The way they landed was then interpreted.*

CHINA DOES NOT have a single religion. Instead Chinese religion is made up of four separate religions and philosophies (ways of thinking). The main three are Confucianism, Buddhism and Taoism. Together, they are known as the *San-chiao* (the three ways). The fourth is the popular folk religion practised throughout the country. The Chinese practise all these religions in their daily lives, picking out those bits that seem most helpful or useful at the time. Few people follow just one.

The first way, Confucianism, is based on the practice of divination (foretelling the future). This is explained in five books, all compiled long before the birth of Confucius. The books are the *I Ching* (*Book of Changes*), the *Shih Ching* (*Book of Poetry*), the *Shu Ching* (*Book of History*), the *Li Chin* (*Book of Rites*) and the *Ch'un-ch'iu* (*Spring and Autumn Annals*). Confucius's own teachings are contained in the *Four Books of Confucianism*. Together these books produce a code of good behaviour for people to follow, rather than a formal religion for them to worship. Followers of Confucius can believe in any god or none.

▲ GOOD WORK
Confucius expected farmers to work hard and produce food for their family and country. Many Chinese festivals celebrate farmers' closeness to the land and their success in getting the harvest in.

Confucius tried to balance the opposing forces of *yin* (darkness) and *yang* (light) in the universe. He stressed the need for order and respect on Earth so that there will be a harmonious balance between heaven, Earth and human beings. To achieve this, people have to learn from the past to see how they should behave today. Confucius ignored existing religious beliefs and stressed instead the importance of serving other people. He said

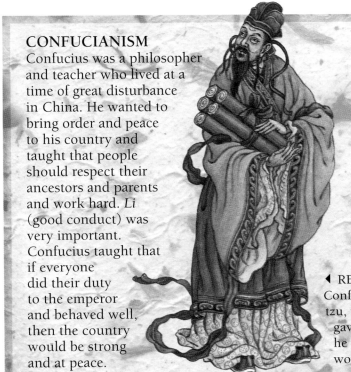

CONFUCIANISM
Confucius was a philosopher and teacher who lived at a time of great disturbance in China. He wanted to bring order and peace to his country and taught that people should respect their ancestors and parents and work hard. *Li* (good conduct) was very important. Confucius taught that if everyone did their duty to the emperor and behaved well, then the country would be strong and at peace.

◄ RELIGIOUS RULER
Confucius's Chinese name, K'ung Fu-tzu, means 'master king.' His parents gave him this name because, when he was born, it was foretold that he would be a king without a crown.

▲ CHINESE TEMPLE
Confucius did not found a religion, but throughout China, shrines and temples were erected in his honour. Confucianism became the state religion.

▼ LOOKING
FORWARD
*Children are very
important in Chinese
life. They represent the
future of the family. In
the Chinese language,
the character for 'good'
(hao) shows a mother
and child, representing
harmony and fertility.*

▶ CONSULTING
THE I CHING
*The I Ching consists of 64
hexagrams (six lines) made up of
broken (yin) or unbroken (yang)
lines. Users draw stalks from a
container, and throw them to the
ground. Then, they consult the I
Ching, compare the way that their
sticks have fallen to what is in the
book and see what they foretell.*

that people should not do anything to other people that they would not like others to do to them. Above all, he taught that it was pointless to worship a god, or honour your ancestors, if you did not serve other people first. The second and fourth ways, Taoism and folk religions, are described on the next page. The third way, Buddhism, has already been described. Together, all four ways showed people how to live their lives as good citizens and therefore keep a balance between *yin* and *yang* in their lives.

▲ EMPEROR TEAON-KWANG
The Chinese believed that the very first Chinese emperors were gods and that their successors had a mandate (approval) from heaven. Emperors were worshipped and treated with great respect.

▼ BELL
Once, when Confucius heard a bell ringing, he decided to give up worldly comforts and live on rice and water for three months as he meditated. To this day, the Chinese believe that bells calm the mind and help clear thinking.

Key Dates

- c.3000BC The *I Ching* is written down by Wen Wang.

- 500sBC Life of Lao-Tzu.

- 551BC Confucius is born.

- c.495–485BC Confucius travels to neighbouring states in the hope of realizing his ideals.

- 479BC Confucius dies.

- 221BC China is united for the first time under Emperor Qin Shi Huangdi.

- 202BC–AD220 Under the Han dynasty, Confucianism becomes the official religion of China.

- AD100s Buddhism reaches China.

Taoism

▲ YIN AND YANG
Yin and yang depend on each other and intertwine. The force of yin represents darkness, water and the female aspect of things. Its opposite, yang, represents light, activity, air and maleness.

THE SECOND WAY of Chinese religion, alongside Confucianism and Buddhism, is Taoism. *Tao* means way, or path, and Taoists believe that there is a life force running through the natural world like a path. Taoists follow this path because it is the natural way and they do not struggle against it. The path is sometimes called the watercourse way, because like a river of water, the path flows in one direction. Like water, it is both powerful and life-giving. Taoists go with the flow of life. Taoist belief is summed up in the saying "Tao never acts, yet there is nothing that is not done."

The legendary founder of Taoism, Lao-tzu, lived at about the same time as Confucius, but little is known about him. He is supposed to be the author of the *Tao Te Ching*, one of the two major works of Taoism. The other is the *Chuang Tzu*.

From these books, two kinds of Taoism have developed – popular and philosophical. The popular form is concerned with religion and includes many gods, goddesses and spirits. Believers seek their help against the many demons that live in the world. They also use ritual and magic to capture the *Te* (power) that brings enlightenment and, they hope, immortality.

Philosophical Taoism is much more mystical and peaceful than religious Taoism. Followers gain an understanding of the Tao by meditation and control of their bodies. They attempt to live in harmony with the Tao. They believe that the body, mind and environment are closely linked and affect each other.

◀ LAO-TZU
The legendary founder of Taoism lived in China in about 500BC. He was probably a scholar. One day he travelled on his ox to a border post, where he was asked to write down his teachings. He did and the book he wrote is known as the Tao Te Ching. After writing it, Lao-Tzu disappeared and was never heard of again.

THE FOURTH WAY – CHINESE FOLK RELIGION
Popular religion in China is very festive, with everybody joining in parades and events. It is concerned with caring for dead ancestors and achieving a balance between the forces of *yin* and *yang*. The art of Feng Shui helps in this. Feng Shui is the practice of placing objects, buildings and even people in the best place to catch the currents of *ch'i* as they circulate.

▼ CHINESE DRAGON
People dressed as dragons, lions and other animals parade through the streets to celebrate Chinese New Year. The dragon brings happiness and good luck and represents the generous spirit of New Year.

▼ FORTUNE COOKIE
People give each other special biscuits called fortune cookies at New Year. Inside them are pieces of paper with a motto.

This belief is shown in the practice of a form of martial art called t'ai chi. Taoists believe that the body has invisible meridians (channels) that run through it carrying blood and *ch'i* (vital energy). The meridian lines feed the vital organs, such as the heart, and ensure a balance between *yin* and *yang*. If this balance is lost, or the flow of *ch'i* is disrupted, acupuncture needles can be used to rebalance the body and ease the flow of *ch'i*.

Taoism never became a major religion in China, although it gained ground during the 1st century AD. It remained popular until 1949 when the Chinese Communists took power. Communists believe that any religion stops people from working to help themselves, fooling them into just doing what they're told. It is for this reason that the new Chinese government destroyed many of the Taoist temples.

▼ MARTIAL ART
T'ai chi is a form of exercise that focuses the mind and the body. People who practise it draw on the strength of the Earth and the ch'i of the heavens.

▲ RELIGIOUS TAOISM
Taoists believe in three star gods (shown here from the top left). These are the gods of long life, wealth and happiness. Taoists also recognize eight immortals (people who will never die), five of whom are shown here. The immortals show living people how to become immortal themselves.

▼ BURNING MONEY
At a Chinese funeral, mourners burn fake money. The notes are meant as a bribe to the gods of the underworld so they will let the dead person through to heaven.

▼ A HOUSEHOLD SHRINE
Most houses have a shrine dedicated to a god. Popular gods include Fu Hsing, who brings happiness, and Tsai Shen, who brings wealth. Despite Communist disapproval of gods and religion, some homes place a picture of the first Communist leader, Chairman Mao, in pride of place at their shrine.

Chinese New Year

The major festival in China is New Year, which falls between 21 January and 19 February. Each New Year is associated with one of twelve animals.

- 2000 is the Year of the Dragon
- 2001 is the Year of the Snake
- 2002 is the Year of the Horse
- 2003 is the Year of the Goat
- 2004 is the Year of the Monkey
- 2005 is the Year of the Rooster
- 2006 is the Year of the Dog
- 2007 is the Year of the Pig
- 2008 is the Year of the Rat
- 2009 is the Year of the Ox
- 2010 is the Year of the Tiger
- 2011 is the Year of the Rabbit
- 2012 is the Year of the Dragon

Shinto

▲ TORII GATE
Every Shinto shrine is entered through a gate called a torii. The torii separates the shrine from the ordinary world outside. It can be some distance from the shrine itself.

THE ANCIENT RELIGION of Japan is called Shinto (way of the gods). The name was first given to the religion in the AD600s. It comes from the Chinese words *shen* (divine being) and *tao* (way). The religion itself, however, is much older, and dates back to Japanese prehistory, perhaps 1,000 years or more before. No one knows who founded Shinto, because it is so old.

The mysterious origins of Shinto are recorded in two books, the *Kojiki* and *Nihongi*, which were compiled at the beginning of the AD700s. Both books were influenced by Chinese thinking, brought to Japan by Buddhist and Confucian teachers.

Over the years, Shinto became the main religion of Japan, but the Japanese do not follow a single religion. Shinto is practised alongside Confucianism, Taoism, Buddhism and, more recently, Christianity. The Japanese take elements from each as they need them.

In many ways, Shinto is not really a religion. It is better described as a collection of attitudes and values about life and society that all Japanese people share. It emphasized the divinity of the emperor and the need to obey the government. There is no formal doctrine (set of beliefs) and no single book or collection that contains the main ideas of Shinto. However, all followers of Shinto believe in the forces of nature, which make themselves felt in *kami* (gods). *Kamis* live in every living thing. The Japanese

◀ TOSHO-GU SHRINE
Shrines are built to honour the kami *or past emperors. Tosho-gu Shrine in Ueno Park, Tokyo, was built in 1651 to commemorate the shogun (ruler) Tokugawa Ieyasu. The shrine's entrance is lined with lanterns. People go to shrines to escape the noise and pressure of everyday life. Sometimes they hang up little prayers that they have written.*

JAPANESE RELIGION
Shinto is the main religion in Japan, but it is quite common to see Buddhist priests at a Shinto shrine and sometimes temples to Buddha have been built within Shinto shrines. Elements of Confucianism and Taoism are also common in Japanese religion.

▶ HIROHITO
The Japanese believe their first emperor, Jimmu, was descended from Amaterasu, the sun goddess. In 1946 Emperor Hirohito said that he was human and renounced his divinity.

◀ MOUNT FUJI
Almost every mountain in Japan has its own god. Sengen-Sama is the goddess of Mount Fuji, the most famous and distinctive mountain in the country. Every year pilgrims climb the mountain at dawn to watch the sun rise.

worship about eight million different *kami* at national and local shrines. The Japanese consult the *kami* at the shrines, asking them for advice or support, and then they follow their instructions. Festivals and rituals play an important part in Shinto.

During the 1800s, Japan began to update its government and economy with ideas imported from Europe. Japanese citizens were given the freedom to worship as they pleased. However, Shinto remained important because it expressed beliefs that are still held by the Japanese people.

▶ THE SUN GODDESS
Amaterasu was the sun goddess who retired into a cave. The world was plunged into darkness and wicked gods created chaos. The good gods enticed Amaterasu out of the cave by making her curious about what was going on without her. Light and peace were then returned to the world.

▲ PORTABLE SHRINE
At a Shinto festival the kami *(god) leaves the shrine and is carried through the streets in a* mikoshi *(portable shrine), to bless everyone in the community. As they process through the streets, the shrine-bearers shake the* mikoshi *to awaken the* kami.

▲ A REQUEST
Japanese people often buy little plaques called *emas*, which they hang up at the temple or shrine. *Emas* are a request for help from the *kami*. This one asks for luck in love. Others request good health, or success in an exam or job interview.

▼ CHILDREN'S DAY
Carp kites are flown to mark Children's Day each May. The carp is a fish that has a long struggle upstream. This represents the difficult journey through life.

Key Dates

- 660BC According to legend, Japan was unified under the first emperor, Jimmu.

- AD600s Chinese Buddhism and Confucianism reach Japan.

- AD645 Reforms of the emperor decide that he is the Son of Heaven and a descendant of the sun goddess Amaterasu.

- AD700s The key Shinto texts, the *Kojiki* and *Nihongi* are compiled.

- 1945 Shinto loses its status as Japan's official state religion.

- 1946 Emperor Hirohito renounces his divinity.

Judaism

▲ JEWISH LIGHTS
The menorah, *a type of multi-branched candlestick, is a symbol of Judaism. A seven-branched* menorah *stood in King Solomon's temple in Jerusalem.*

JUDAISM IS THE RELIGION of the Jewish people. Jews trace their origins back to Abraham (the Father of Many Nations), who lived in Mesopotamia (modern-day Iraq) more than 4,000 years ago. They believe that God revealed himself to Abraham and promised to make him the father of a great nation. Abraham and his family settled in Canaan (modern-day Israel), and this became the centre of Judaism. As Jews chose or were forced to settle elsewhere, the religion gradually spread. Today there are more than 13 million Jews worldwide, with large numbers in Israel, the USA, and in Russia, Ukraine and other countries of the former USSR.

Judaism was the first great faith to believe that there is only one God. An important statement called the *Shema* (in the *Tenakh*, the Jewish holy book) says "Hear, O Israel: the Lord our God, the Lord is One."

Jews believe that God is the creator of the world, and that he chose their ancestors, the Israelites, to be his special people. He led the Israelites out of slavery in Egypt and brought them to Canaan, the Promised Land. God's holy name is the Hebrew (Jewish) word *Yhwh*, usually written as

▼ THE FERTILE CRESCENT
Most of the events in the Hebrew Bible took place in the region known as the Fertile Crescent. This is a huge arc of fertile land, stretching from the Tigris and Euphrates rivers in Mesopotamia (modern-day Iraq) and through the Jewish homeland of Israel to Egypt.

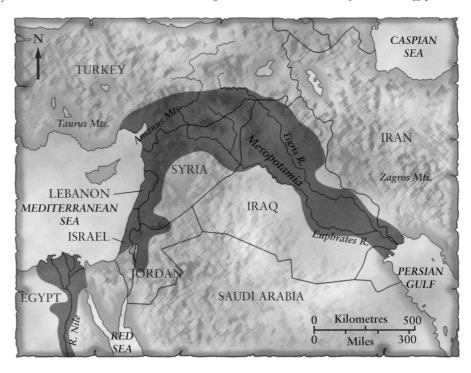

MODERN JEWISH GROUPS

Different customs have evolved in the various Jewish communities around the world. The two main groups are the Orthodox (traditional) Jews and the Reform Jews. Orthodox Jews stick to the traditional way of doing things. They hold their services in Hebrew, follow the ancient food laws, and separate men and women in the synagogue, the Jewish place of worship. Reform Jews reject traditional customs that seem old-fashioned to them. They hold their services in the local language, rather than Hebrew. They modify or discard the food laws, and they allow women to become rabbis.

▶ ETHIOPIAN JEWS
The Falasha are Jews who live in Ethiopia, east Africa. Their ancestors converted to Judaism more than 2,000 years ago. In the 1980s, about 45,000 Falasha emigrated to Israel to escape the war and drought in Ethiopia.

◀ THE TALMUD
Study of the scriptures is an important part of Jewish education. The main books are the Hebrew Bible, or *Tenakh* and the *Talmud*, a book of Jewish laws written in Babylon around 500BC.

Yahweh. Yahweh means 'I am' or 'I am who I am.'

Jews believe that God communicates with people through prophets. The greatest prophet was Moses, to whom God revealed the *Torah*, the first five books of the Bible. The *Torah* contains God's sacred laws, the best-known of which are the Ten Commandments. Keeping these laws is central to the Jewish way of life.

Jews believe that in the future, God will send a Messiah (anointed one), who will right all wrongs, reward good people and punish evil. His arrival will mark the end of history and the beginning of God's kingdom on Earth. Some Jews believe that when this happens the dead will be resurrected (brought back to eternal life). Other Jews believe that when they die their souls will go on living.

▲ THE GREAT FLOOD
According to the Bible, God sent a flood to destroy everything and rid the world of sin. Noah and his family were the only people to survive. Noah built an ark (huge boat), in which he saved his family and the animals.

▶ MODERN ISRAEL
Six million Jews were killed during the Holocaust in World War II. After the war, Jews stepped up their campaign to have their own country, where they could live and worship without threat of persecution. In 1948 the state of Israel was created as a Jewish homeland. Since then, thousands of Jews from all over the world have emigrated to Israel.

▲ RELIGIOUS TEACHER
Rabbis are the spiritual leaders for the Jewish community. They conduct services and teach children about Judaism.

▼ HASIDIC JEWS AT THE WESTERN WALL
Hasidism is a strict form of Judaism that originated in southeast Poland in the 1700s. It was founded by a Jewish scholar called Dov Baer. Hasidic Jews have many special customs. The men wear black suits and hats, and have side curls and beards. *Tzaddiqim* (Hasidic leaders) established new communities after World War II, when many Hasidic Jews were killed. These include the Lubavich sect in New York City.

Key Dates

- c.2166BC Birth of Abraham, the founder of the Jewish nation.

- c.586–537BC Judaism spreads beyond Canaan, when hundreds of Jews are forced into slavery in Babylon.

- c.500BC The *Talmud* is written.

- AD70 The Jewish population spreads throughout the Roman Empire. This is known as the Diaspora (dispersal).

- 1939–45 During World War II, six million Jews are killed by the Nazis during the Holocaust.

- 1948 The state of Israel is founded.

The Chosen People

▲ STAR OF DAVID
The Israeli flag features the six-pointed Star of David, which is a symbol of Judaism. In Hebrew, it is known as the Shield of David because King David had this star on his shield.

THE JEWS BELIEVE that they are God's chosen people. According to the Bible, the story of God's special relationship with the Jews started with Abraham. God asked him and his family to leave his home in Mesopotamia and travel to Canaan (modern-day Israel). In return for Abraham's faith and obedience, God promised that he would become the founder of a great nation, and that his descendants would inherit the land of Canaan. This agreement between God and Abraham is known as the covenant.

Many years later, God made another covenant with his people. Abraham's descendants, the Israelites, were living in slavery in Egypt. God chose Moses to be their leader and to take them out of Egypt to the Promised Land (Canaan). This is known as the Exodus. At Mount Sinai, God gave Moses Ten Commandments and promised to protect his chosen people if they kept these laws.

The journey to the Promised Land took a long time. The Bible says that the Israelites spent 40 years wandering in the wilderness, and that Moses died before they entered Canaan. Under his successor, Joshua, and later leaders, the Israelites gradually captured the land from its existing inhabitants.

The Israelites settled in Canaan, but over the years they stopped obeying God's laws. For this reason God allowed them to be threatened by the Philistines and other enemies. God renewed his covenant with the

▼ THE PROPHET EZEKIEL
Throughout Jewish history, God has spoken through prophets or wise men. Ezekiel was a priest who was deported to Babylon in 586BC. He told his fellow-exiles to keep their faith in God.

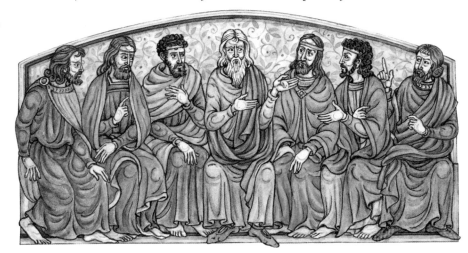

PLACES OF WORSHIP

Jews usually meet to worship at a synagogue. Prayers are held there in the morning, afternoon and evening each day, but many Jews only attend on Saturday, the Jewish Sabbath holy day. Worship is often led by the rabbi. It includes prayers and *Tenakh* readings.

▶ TEMPLE REMAINS
The Western Wall is all that is left of the temple in Jerusalem. It is a sacred place, where Jewish people go to pray. Some write prayers on pieces of paper, which they tuck between the blocks of stone in the wall.

◀ THE TEMPLE IN JERUSALEM
King Solomon built the first temple in Jerusalem, which became the centre of Jewish worship. His temple was destroyed by the Babylonians in 587BC, but later temples were built on the same site, the last by King Herod. This was destroyed by the Romans in AD70. The Western Wall is all that remains of it.

Israelites through David. He promised to make David a great king and to protect his people if they obeyed his laws. God told David to build a magnificent temple in Jerusalem as a sign of this covenant. The temple was eventually built by David's son, Solomon.

Hundreds of years later, in 586BC, Canaan was seized by the Babylonians, who took many Jews away to Babylon as slaves. In the Bible, the *Psalms* (songs) tell how the Jews missed their homeland during this period, but how they believed that God would return them to the Promised Land. Eventually Babylon was defeated by the Persians and the Jews returned home.

Jews today look back on their history. As they did in the past, they strongly believe that if they obey God, he will continue to look after them.

◀ KING SOLOMON
For much of their history, the Jews were ruled by a series of kings. King Solomon, the son of David, was famous for his wisdom. He built the first temple in Jerusalem.

▲ DAVID AND GOLIATH
As a shepherd boy, David killed the giant Goliath with just a stone and a sling. He later became the king of Israel. David established Jerusalem as the capital city of his kingdom.

▼ HOUSE OF WORSHIP
A synagogue is a place where Jews meet to pray and to study the *Tenakh*. All synagogues are built facing in the direction of Jerusalem. There is usually a cupboard in the end wall, known as the Ark of the Covenant, which contains the *Torah* scrolls. In Orthodox synagogues, men and women sit in separate areas.

▲ INCENSE BURNER
Incense is sometimes burned in Jewish synagogues. The smoke symbolizes people's prayers, rising up to God.

Key Dates

- c.2166BC Birth of Abraham.
- c.1700BC The Israelites move to Egypt to escape a famine.
- c.1446BC Moses leads the Israelites out of Egypt.
- c.1406BC The Israelites enter Canaan (the Promised Land).
- c.960BC Solomon completes the temple in Jerusalem.
- c.930BC The kingdom divides into Judah and Israel.
- c.586BC The Babylonians destroy the temple and enslave many Jews.
- c.537–445BC The Jews return to Judah and rebuild the temple.

Jewish Scriptures

THE HEBREW BIBLE IS the sacred book of the Jewish people. It also forms the first half of the Christian Bible, where it is known as the Old Testament. It tells the story of the Jewish people and their special relationship with God. The events it describes took place over a period of more than 2,000 years.

The Hebrew Bible is not one single book, but a collection of books written over many centuries by many different authors. It contains books of law, history, poetry and prophecy. The Jews group the books of their Bible into three main sections: the *Torah* (law), the *Nevi'im* (prophets) and the *Ketuvim* (writings).

The most important part of Hebrew Bible is the first five books, known as the *Torah*, or law. It contains the Ten Commandments and other laws given by God to Moses. The *Torah* also tells the story of the Jewish people from the time of their founder, Abraham, to the time of Moses. One of the most important themes of the *Torah*

▲ SPICE BOX
At the end of the Sabbath some Jews breathe in spices from a spice box to keep the sweet smell of the Sabbath with them all week.

◀ THE SHOFAR
The shofar is a trumpet made from a ram's horn. In ancient times, the Israelites used it to rally their warriors in battle and to summon people to worship. The shofar is still blown in synagogues at Yom Kippur (the Jewish fast) and Rosh Hashanah (Jewish New Year).

RITES AND RITUALS
Each week Jews keep their holy day, the Sabbath, the day of rest as ordered by God in the Ten Commandments. This starts with a family meal on Friday evening and lasts until sunset on Saturday. Throughout the year, Jews celebrate a number of festivals. Some of them commemorate specific events in Jewish history, such as the Exodus from Egypt. Other festivals are connected to the seasons and the events of the farming year.

▼ THE HAGADAH
At Pesach (Passover), Jewish families share a special meal, called the *seder*. During the meal they read from a part of the *Talmud* called the *Hagadah*. It tells how the Israelites escaped from Egypt.

▼ SUKKOT
At the autumn festival of Sukkot (the festival of booths) Jews remember the 40 years that they spent in the wilderness. They make booths (tents) out of leaves and branches to symbolize the ones that they used in the desert.

◀ TORAH COVERS
Each synagogue has a copy of the Torah, written on a long scroll. Jews believe that the Torah is too sacred to touch, so the reader uses a pointer to keep their place in the text. The Torah is often stored in a decorated, protective cover. Popular images on Torah covers include the lion, which represents the tribe of Judah, and the menorah.

▼ KOSHER FOOD
The Torah contains laws about food, which forbid Jews to eat certain types of meat, such as pork or rabbit, or to eat the blood of animals. Another law states that they cannot eat meat and milk in the same meal. Many Jews buy their food, especially meat, from special shops where it has been prepared according to the food laws. Food prepared in this way is called kosher.

is God's covenant (agreement), made first with Abraham and his descendants, and then again with Moses. This covenant showed the Jews that they were God's chosen people.

After the *Torah* is the section of the Bible known as the *Nebi'im*. This is made up of eight books, believed to have been written by Jewish prophets, including Samuel, Isaiah and Ezekiel. The *Nevi'im* continues the history of the Jews, from their conquest of the Promised Land up to the fall of the Jewish kings. In their books, the prophets explained the meaning of these events and warned the Jews about the dangers of disobeying God.

The remaining 11 books of the Hebrew Bible are called the *Ketuvim*. This section contains books of wisdom, poetry, prophecy and history. Among them is the *Book of Psalms*. This is a collection of hymns and prayers, many of which were written by King David.

▲ COMING OF AGE
Bar Mitzvah is the ceremony at which a boy becomes an adult member of the Jewish community. It happens when he is 13 years old and takes place in the synagogue. As part of the ceremony, the boy reads aloud from the *Torah*. Some Jews have a similar service to mark girls' entry into adulthood. This is called Bat Mitzvah.

▼ DECEMBER FESTIVAL
Hanukkah celebrates how the Jews reclaimed the temple from the Greek rulers in 164BC. The temple's lamp had only enough oil for one day, but burned for eight days. On each of the eight days of the festival, Jewish families light one more candle on a *menorah*. They do this using the ninth candle, or *shamash*, in the centre of the candlestick.

The Jewish Year

- February/March – Purim (celebrating how Esther saved the Jews from the Persians)

- March/April – Pesach or Passover (commemorating the Exodus, when the angel of death killed every first-born Egyptian, but passed over the Israelites)

- May/June – Shavuot (marking the giving of the law to Moses)

- September/October – Rosh Hashanah (Jewish New Year)

- September/October – Yom Kippur (the Day of Atonement)

- September/October – Sukkot

- December – Hanukkah

Christianity

THE FOUNDER OF CHRISTIANITY was Jesus Christ, a Jewish teacher and healer who lived in what is now Israel during the first century AD. His followers steadily grew in number. In the AD300s the Roman emperor, Constantine, decreed that Christianity should be tolerated throughout his empire. An important figure around that time was Augustine, who was bishop of Hippo (in modern-day Algeria, Africa) from AD396 until AD430. Augustine developed Christian thought in his *Confessions*, mixing them with Greek ideas. His interpretation of Christianity spread throughout Europe.

From the 1500s, as Europeans explored other continents, they took Christianity with them. Today Christians live on every continent of the globe. They total almost two billion, making Christianity the world's biggest religion.

Christians believe in one God. They believe that Jesus Christ was the Messiah promised in the Old Testament. The Christian God has three parts, known as the Holy Trinity. The Trinity consists of God the Father, God the Son (Jesus) and God the Holy Spirit.

Christians believe that God came to Earth in the form of a man, Jesus. He showed

▲ THE CROSS
Jesus was crucified (put to death on a cross), but Christians believe he rose from the dead. This has made the cross a symbol of Jesus's sacrifice. Christians see it as a symbol of victory and hope, too.

▲ THE VIRGIN MARY
The Bible says that Jesus's mother, Mary, was a virgin. The power of the Holy Spirit made her pregnant, so that Jesus could be born as a human being.

THE CHRISTIAN CHURCH
The first Christian Church was the Catholic (universal) Church, with the Pope at its head. In the AD1000s there was disagreement about the use of icons (holy pictures). This led to a split between the Catholic Church in Rome and the Orthodox Church, based in Constantinople. This is called the Great Schism (split). The Protestant churches were founded in the 1500s. This period is called the Reformation.

▲ MARTIN LUTHER
Luther was a German monk. He felt the Catholic Church abused its position of power. In protest, he founded the first Protestant church in the 1520s.

◀ ST PETER'S BASILICA
The Pope lives in the Vatican, a tiny country within the city of Rome. The Pope's church is St Peter's, begun in 1506 by Pope Julius II.

▶ JOHN CALVIN
Calvin set up a Protestant church in Switzerland. Like Luther, he tried to get rid of church traditions and simply follow the teachings of the Bible.

▼ ORTHODOX ICONS
Orthodox churches are usually full of beautiful icons. These are religious pictures or statues of Jesus, Mary, or the saints.

people how to confess the things they had done wrong in the past and have a fresh start with God. During his lifetime Jesus gathered a large body of followers. This alarmed the Romans, who occupied what is now Israel, and also the Jewish religious authorities, who feared Jesus was damaging their own power base. Jesus was put on trial and sentenced to death by crucifixion. When Jesus died, followers of Jesus believe that he paid the price for everyone's sins. According to the Bible, three days after his death, Jesus rose from the dead. Christians believe that when they die, they can look forward to eternal life in heaven.

Jesus said in the Bible that he is still with all Christians in spirit, and that he will come back at the end of the world to judge all people. Those who have faith in him will be saved and go to heaven. Those who have not will be banished to hell.

Jesus promised his disciples (followers) that after he was gone he would send a helper for them, the Holy Spirit. Christians believe this Spirit is still active in the world today.

▶ THE ASCENSION
Jesus appeared to his followers on many occasions in the 40 days following his resurrection, when he came back to life. Then one day he was taken up into heaven before his disciples' eyes. This event is known as the Ascension.

Roman Catholic regions

Protestant regions

Orthodox regions

N

NORWAY
SWEDEN
SCOTLAND
NORTH SEA
Dublin
Hamburg
IRELAND
WALES
ENGLAND
R. Rhine
HOLY ROMAN EMPIRE
BOHEMIA
Paris
R. Danube
Vienna
ATLANTIC OCEAN
R. Loire
FRANCE
SPAIN
PORTUGAL
Madrid
Rome
PAPAL STATES
R. Tagus
0 Kilometres 750
0 Miles 500
MEDITERRANEAN SEA

◀ EUROPE IN THE 1500S
During the Reformation, northern Europe became mostly Protestant, while southern Europe remained mostly Catholic. Most Orthodox Christians live in Russia and parts of eastern Europe, such as Greece and the Balkans.

Key Dates

- c.AD30 Birth of the Christian Church. Jesus's disciples start to preach the Christian message.

- AD313 Emperor Constantine grants tolerance of Christianity. It eventually becomes the official religion of the Roman Empire.

- 1054 The Orthodox Church breaks away in the Great Schism.

- 1517 Martin Luther publicly criticizes the Catholic Church and starts the Reformation. Protestant churches are founded.

- 2000 Christians celebrate the millennium, 2,000 years after the traditional birth date of Jesus.

The Life of Jesus

▲ JESUS
All that we know about Jesus's life comes from the accounts in the four gospels, the books of the Bible written specifically about Jesus.

▶ PARABLES
Jesus often told parables (stories about everyday life) to teach people about God in a way they could understand and remember. One of his most famous parables is the story of the good samaritan. It tells the story of a man who was helped by the one person he thought was his enemy.

JESUS CHRIST WAS BORN IN about 6 or 7BC in Judah (modern-day Israel), which was then a province of the Roman Empire. His mother was Mary, a young Jewish woman from Nazareth.

According to the Bible, the Angel Gabriel appeared to Mary and told her that she would have a child who would be God's son and the saviour of the world.

We know very little about Jesus' childhood, except that he lived in Nazareth and was brought up as a Jew. The Bible picks up the story when Jesus was in his early 30s. He was baptized in the River Jordan and spent

WEEKLY WORSHIP

Christians gather together to worship God on Sunday and at other important festivals. They usually meet in a church, but some groups meet in people's homes. The most important form of Christian worship is the service known as communion, mass, or the Eucharist. At holy communion, Christians share bread and wine as Jesus did with his disciples at the Last Supper. Christian worship includes prayers, readings from the Bible, and singing religious songs called hymns.

◀ NOTRE-DAME CATHEDRAL
Huge cathedrals were built in Europe during the Middle Ages. One of the most beautiful is the Cathedral of Notre-Dame (Our Lady), in Paris, which was begun in 1163. It has three stained-glass windows.

▲ MODERN CATHEDRAL
Not all cathedrals are old. The Cathedral of Christ the King, in Liverpool, England, dates from 1967.

◀ A PARISH CHURCH
Most Christians worship at a small local church, with members of their parish (community).

40 days fasting in the desert in preparation for his work. Then he travelled around the country, teaching people about God, healing the sick and performing miracles. He was accompanied by a group of 12 disciples (followers). Jesus told people that God's kingdom was coming and that they should ask God's forgiveness so they could be saved. Jesus became very popular and vast crowds of people came to hear him preach. However, he faced opposition from the Jewish religious authorities, who saw him as a threat.

After three years, Jesus travelled to Jerusalem for the Jewish festival of Pesach (Passover). According to the Bible he rode a donkey into the city, cheered on by crowds who threw palm branches in his path. Later in the week, Jesus and his disciples ate *seder* (the Pesach meal) together. This is now known as the Last Supper. Jesus shared bread and wine with his disciples. Later that night, Jesus was arrested, tried and found guilty by the religious authorities. The Roman governor of the province, Pontius Pilate, sentenced him to death. The following day, Jesus was forced to carry a wooden cross through the streets of Jerusalem to a place outside the city walls, where he was crucified. He died in the afternoon, and was buried by his friends and followers.

Three days later Jesus's followers discovered that his tomb was empty. An angel told them that Jesus was alive again. Jesus himself appeared to his astonished disciples on many occasions over the next few weeks. Forty days later, he was taken up into heaven. This marked the end of his life on Earth, but Christians believe that Jesus is still alive in heaven.

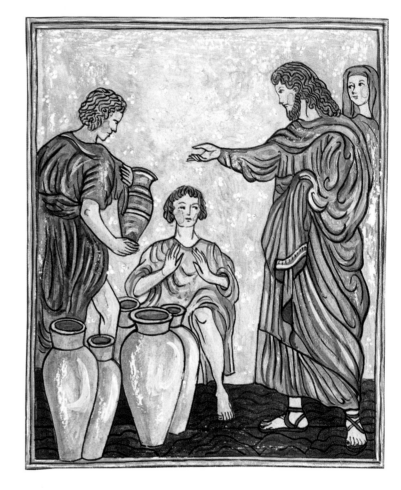

▲ THE WEDDING AT CANA
In the three years of his teaching, Jesus performed many miracles. His first was to turn jars of water into wine at a wedding. Jesus healed many people, and even brought a dead man, Lazarus, back to life. He also used miracles to demonstrate his power over nature, for example by calming a storm.

▲ HOLY COMMUNION
The bread and wine that Christians receive at communion represent the body and blood of Jesus. At the Last Supper, Jesus told his disciples to think of bread and wine in this way.

▼ FORMS OF WORSHIP
There are many styles of Christian worship. The Baptist Church, founded around 1611, is known for its lively services. Baptists celebrate Jesus with joyful singing and even dancing.

Key Dates

- c.6–7BC Jesus is born in Bethlehem.His family flees to Egypt to escape King Herod.
- c.4BC King Herod dies and Jesus's family returns to Nazareth.
- c.AD5–6 Jesus visits the temple at Jerusalem with his family where he is dedicated to God.
- c.AD28 Jesus is baptized in the River Jordan and starts his public teaching.
- c.AD30 Jesus is crucified in Jerusalem, but is resurrected after three days. About forty days later he ascends into heaven.

The Christian Scriptures

THE CHRISTIAN HOLY BOOK is the Bible. Christians believe that although the Bible was written by people, it was inspired by God. It is a collection of books written by different authors. These books are divided into two sections, the Old and New Testaments. The Old Testament consists of the Jewish scriptures. The New Testament deals with the life and teachings of Jesus Christ and the story of the early Christian church. All 27 books in the New Testament were written by early followers of Jesus, roughly between AD45 and AD97.

The first four books of the New Testament are the gospels of Matthew, Mark, Luke and John. The word gospel means 'good news' and refers to the good news that Jesus was the long-awaited Messiah. Together the gospels tell the story of Jesus's life. All four of the gospel writers were closely involved with Jesus or with his followers. Matthew and John were two of Jesus's disciples. Mark was probably a translator for Peter, another of the 12 disciples. Luke was a friend of Paul. Paul was not a disciple. He was a Jew who had persecuted the Christians but converted to Christianity after seeing a vision on the road to Damascus. After this, Paul travelled widely spreading the Christian message.

Each of the gospels tells the life of Jesus from a different viewpoint. All four concentrate on Jesus's ministry, his time teaching in Galilee, and on the events of the last week of his life.

The fifth book of the New Testament, *The Acts of the*

▲ GUTENBERG BIBLE
In the Middle Ages, when all books had to be copied out by hand, Christian monks produced some beautiful Bibles. The first printed edition was the Gutenberg Bible of 1455.

◀ ST ANDREW AND ST JAMES
The first four disciples that Jesus recruited were Peter, Andrew, James and John. After Jesus's death, they carried on preaching his message. Some died for their religion. King Herod Agrippa I of Judah had James beheaded around AD44 and Andrew was crucified in modern-day Turkey in the AD60s.

THE CHRISTIAN YEAR
Christians celebrate many festivals. Most commemorate events in Jesus's life. In some churches, saints are celebrated on the particular days dedicated to them. Festivals are marked with special church services and with other customs, such as giving Christmas presents or Easter eggs.

▲ EASTER EGGS
In some countries it is traditional to give and receive eggs at Easter, as a symbol of new life. Easter eggs may be real, or made of wood or chocolate.

◀ THE NATIVITY
At Christmas, Christian homes and churches often display models of the nativity, Jesus's birth in the stable in Bethlehem.

▲ PALM SUNDAY
Shortly before his death, Jesus rode into Jerusalem on a donkey. He was greeted by crowds of people, who laid palm branches in his path. Christians remember this event on Palm Sunday. At some churches, small crosses made of palm leaves are handed out to worshippers.

◀ RUINS AT EPHESUS
*Paul was one of the first church leaders to
see that the good news about Jesus was
meant for all, not just Jews. He went on
four journeys around the Mediterranean,
telling people about Jesus and founding
Christian churches in cities such as
Ephesus in Turkey, and Corinth, in Greece.*

Apostles, was written by Luke, the author of the third gospel. It tells
what happened in the 30 years after Jesus's ascension into heaven.
Acts describes the missionary work of the apostles, Jesus's specially
appointed helpers, the life of the early Christian church, and Paul's travels.

The next 21 books are letters from the early Christian leaders to the
newly founded churches, giving them advice and encouragement. Paul
is believed to have written 13 of the letters. Other authors include the
disciple Peter and Jesus's brother, James.

The final book of the Bible is the *Book of Revelation*. The writer,
John, who may be the same John that wrote the fourth gospel, describes
what will happen at the end of the world.

▲ A FRANCISCAN FRIAR
*Monks or friars try to spread the Christian
message by setting a good example. Francis,
who later became a saint, founded his order
of monks in 1209. The Franciscans live in
poverty and in harmony with nature.*

▶ PENTECOST
A few days after Jesus
had ascended into
heaven, his disciples
gathered together on
the Jewish festival of
Shavuot. The Bible says
that they suddenly heard
a sound like rushing
wind. They saw tongues
of flame that came to
rest on each of them.
They were all filled with
the power of the Holy
Spirit and began to
speak in tongues (other
languages). Christians
celebrate this event at
the festival of Pentecost,
or Whitsun.

Christian Festivals

- 25 December – Christmas
  (celebrates Jesus's birth)

- March/April – Lent (a 40-day
  fast that ends on Easter Sunday)

- March/April – Maundy Thursday
  (held the Thursday before Easter
  to celebrate the Last Supper)

- March/April – Good Friday
  (marks the crucifixion of Jesus)

- March/April – Easter Sunday
  (celebrates Jesus's resurrection)

- May/June – Pentecost or
  Whitsun (celebrates when
  the disciples received the
  Holy Spirit)

Islam

▲ SACRED SYMBOL
The hilal *(crescent moon and star) is the symbol of Islam. It reminds Muslims that they follow a lunar calendar (a calendar based on the movements of the Moon), and that Allah created the stars. The* hilal *appears on the flags of some Muslim countries, including Pakistan, Singapore and Turkey.*

ISLAM WAS FOUNDED by the prophet Muhammad. It began in the cities of al-Madinah (Medina) and Makkah (Mecca) in modern-day Saudi Arabia in about AD620. Muhammad received revelations from Allah (God) and began to preach his message.

Muhammad died in AD632, and within a few years the peoples of the Arabian peninsula had converted to Islam. The new religion soon had followers as far west as the Atlantic coast of Africa and as far east as India. Today, Islam is the world's second-largest religion, with more than a billion followers spread over almost every country.

The word Islam means 'surrender to the peace of Allah.' Muslims (followers of Islam) give themselves up to Allah's will. They believe that Allah is the one God, and that Muhammad was Allah's messenger.

Muslims believe that Allah sent many prophets (messengers) before sending Muhammad. These include holy men recognized by Jews and Christians, such as Adam, Ibrahim (Abraham), Musa (Moses), Dawud (David) and Isa (Jesus). Muhammad received revelations from Allah through the Angel Jibril (Gabriel) from the age of 40. He told his followers about these revelations. They were eventually written down in the Islamic holy book, the Qur'an.

Muslims believe that their faith is the final revelation of Allah. Every aspect of Muslim life is governed by the Five Pillars of Islam, duties that unite Muslims all over the world into a single community.

▶ THE SACRED KA'BAH
The Great Mosque at Makkah is set around the Ka'bah, a square building made of grey stone. In its eastern corner is the Black Stone. Muslims believe this fell to Earth as a sign of the covenant (agreement) between Allah and the prophet Ibrahim. Muslims believe that Ibrahim built the Ka'bah.

THE FIVE PILLARS OF ISLAM
Islam rests on five duties that all Muslims must obey and carry out. These are called the Five Pillars (supports) of Islam. They are based on the Qur'an and the actions of Muhammad. They give a sense of purpose to every Muslim's life.

◀ SHAHADAH
The first pillar is *shahadah*. This is the Muslim statement of faith – that Allah is the one true God, and that Muhammad was his prophet. This belief is stated each day in the call to prayer.

◀ SALAH
The second pillar is *salah*, the prayers that Muslims say five times a day. Wherever they are in the world, Muslims face towards the sacred Ka'bah in Makkah when they pray.

▼ CHARITY SCHOOL, OMAN
Every Muslim must give one-fortieth of his or her annual income to charities such as this religious school. This is called *zakat*, and is the third pillar.

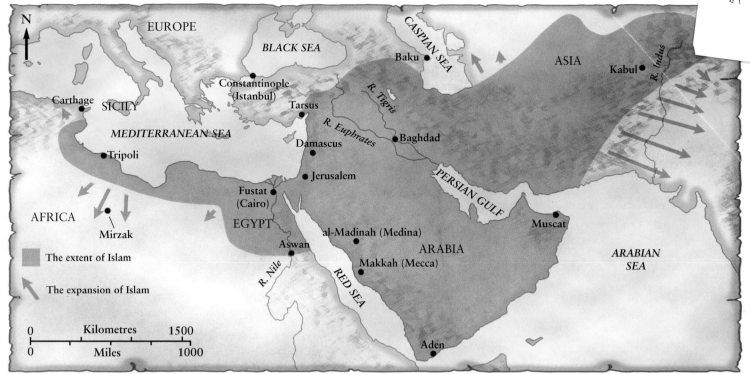

N

EUROPE
BLACK SEA
Baku
CASPIAN SEA
ASIA
Kabul
R. Indus
Constantinople (Istanbul)
Tarsus
R. Tigris
Carthage
SICILY
MEDITERRANEAN SEA
R. Euphrates
Baghdad
Damascus
Tripoli
Jerusalem
PERSIAN GULF
Fustat (Cairo)
EGYPT
AFRICA
Mirzak
al-Madinah (Medina)
Muscat
Aswan
Makkah (Mecca)
ARABIA
ARABIAN SEA

The extent of Islam

The expansion of Islam

R. Nile
RED SEA
Aden

| 0 | Kilometres | 1500 |
| 0 | Miles | 1000 |

▶ HOLY SITE

Al-Aqsa (the Dome of the Rock) in Jerusalem is where Muhammad ascended into heaven in AD619 to meet Allah. It is sacred to Jews and Christians, too, as the ancient site of Solomon's temple. Other holy Muslim sites are the Great Mosque at Makkah and the tomb of Muhammad at al-Madinah.

▲ THE ISLAMIC WORLD

Islam began in the cities of Makkah and al-Madinah. It became the chief religion of the Arabian peninsula, spreading into Persia (modern-day Iran), Mesopotamia (modern-day Iraq) and North Africa. During the 1100s and 1200s, Christian knights known as Crusaders recaptured Jerusalem from Muslim control, but they failed to hold their gains for long.

▼ ID-UL-FITR

The fourth pillar is *sawm* (fasting). During the month of Ramadan, Muslims do not eat or drink during daylight hours. Muslims celebrate the end of Ramadan with a feast. They call this festival Id-ul-Fitr.

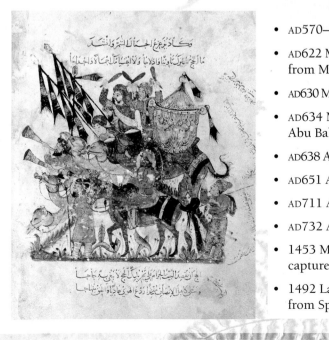

Key Dates

- AD570–632 Life of Muhammad.

- AD622 Muhammad's hijrah (flight) from Makkah to al-Madinah.

- AD630 Muhammad conquers Makkah.

- AD634 Muhammad's successor, Abu Bakr, conquers Arabia.

- AD638 Arab armies capture Jerusalem.

- AD651 Arab armies overrun Persia.

- AD711 Arab armies reach India.

- AD732 Arab armies conquer Spain.

- 1453 Muslim Ottoman Turks capture Constantinople.

- 1492 Last Muslim armies retreat from Spain.

▶ TO BE A PILGRIM

During their lifetime all healthy Muslims must make at least one *hajj* (pilgrimage) to Makkah during the 12th month of the Islamic year. The *hajj* is the fifth pillar.

The Life of Muhammad

▲ MIHRAB TO MAKKAH
Makkah is sacred to Muslims because it was there, in AD610, that Muhammad had his first vision of the Angel Jibril. Muslim mosques, such as this one at Aleppo, Syria, always feature a mihrab *(an alcove in the wall that shows the direction of Makkah).*

MUHAMMAD WAS BORN in the Arabian city of Makkah in AD570. He was orphaned as a child and brought up by his grandfather and then his uncle. He worked as a desert trader and in AD595 married Khadijah, a wealthy widow. Muhammad became wealthy and well-respected in the city. However, he was increasingly concerned about the worship of pagan gods at the Ka'bah, the sacred house said to have been built by Ibrahim. Muhammad used to go and pray and meditate in the mountains at Hira outside Makkah. In AD610 he was meditating when the

▶ HARUN AL-RASHID
In AD750 the Abbasid Dynasty took control of the Muslim world. They moved the capital from Damascus (in modern-day Syria) to Baghdad (in modern-day Iraq). Under Caliph (leader) Harun Al-Rashid (AD786–809), Baghdad became the centre of Islamic arts and learning.

ISLAMIC WORSHIP
The centre of the Islamic religion is the mosque. It is a space for prayer, worship, teaching and study. It also acts as a community centre for local Muslims. The main weekly service is usually held on Friday afternoon, but the mosque is open throughout the week for constant prayer and study.

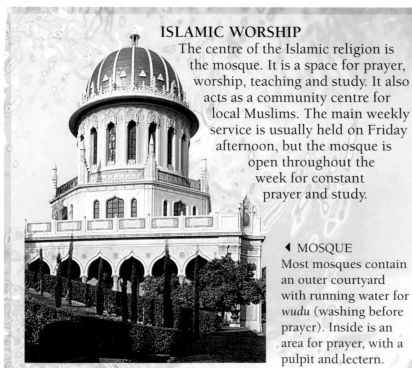

◀ MOSQUE
Most mosques contain an outer courtyard with running water for *wudu* (washing before prayer). Inside is an area for prayer, with a pulpit and lectern.

▶ THE MINARET
Each mosque has a minaret (tower). A man called a *mu'adhin* or *muezzin* climbs it five times each day and calls Muslims to prayer.

▼ WOMEN AT WORSHIP
Muslim men and women pray separately. Most women worship at home, but some mosques have special areas reserved for women.

as the *hijrah* (emigration), marks the start of the Islamic Era. All Muslim calendars are dated AH (*Anno Hegirae* is Latin for 'year of the *hijrah*'). The year AD2000 is 1421AH in the Muslim calendar.

By AD630 Muhammad had a strong enough following to return in triumph to Makkah. He forgave his former enemies,

Angel Jibril appeared to him and told him he would be Allah's messenger. Muhammad had further revelations for the rest his life. These include his famous night journey of AD619, when Jibril took him to Jersualem and then up to heaven to meet Allah. Muhammad tried to preach Allah's message to the people of Makkah, but they did not want to listen. In AD622 Muhammad fled the city and moved to al-Madinah. The people there did listen, and al-Madinah became the first Islamic city. For this reason, Muhammad's flight from Makkah, known

and many became Muslims. After Muhammad's death in AD632, Islam became the major religion of the Middle East and North Africa. However it soon split into two groups, Sunnis and Shi'ahs. The two groups have many beliefs in common but the Sunnis believed that Muhammad's successors should be chosen by the Muslim community. The Shi'ahs believed that only the descendants of his cousin and son-in-law, Ali, could follow him. Most Muslims today are Sunnis. Ten per cent are Shi'ahs, and they live mainly in Iran.

◀ IMAM
The main official at the mosque is called the *imam* (chief). He leads the prayers. Sermons are read by the *khatib* (preacher).

▶ SAJJADA
Muslims use a *sajjada* (prayer mat) to make sure that they pray on a clean space. Many mats have a picture of a mosque. Some feature an inbuilt compass so that the user always knows the direction of Makkah and which way to face as he prays.

Key Dates

- AD595 Muhammad marries Khadijah, a wealthy widow.

- AD610 Muhammad's vision of Jibral in a cave on Mt Hira.

- AD619 Muhammad's Night Journey with Jibril to Jerusalem.

- AD622 Muhammad's *hijrah*.

- AD630 Muhammad captures Makkah.

- AD632 Muhammad dies in Makkah and is buried in al-Madinah.

- AD632 Abu Bakr becomes the first caliph (Muslim ruler).

- AD680 Sunni/Shi'ah split.

The Qur'an

▲ CALLIGRAPHY
Muslims are forbidden to depict Allah or Muhammad in paintings. They decorate the Qur'an with geometric or floral designs and with intricate calligraphy (writing). This lettering is the Arabic script for 'Allah.'

MUHAMMAD TOLD his followers all the teachings that Allah had passed on to him through the Angel Jibral. They learned his revelations by heart and dictated them to scribes, who wrote them down in what became the Qur'an, which means 'revelation.' Muslims believe that earlier messages from Allah to his prophets had been corrupted or ignored. They believe that the Qur'an is the true word of Allah. As it was spoken by Muhammad in Arabic, the Qur'an can only be written and recited in Arabic, regardless of the language of the believer. Muslims believe that the Qur'an is perfect and therefore it cannot be translated into any other language, only interpreted.

Copies of the Qur'an are always beautifully illustrated. Muslims believe that making the

word of Allah beautiful is in itself an act of worship.

The Qur'an is divided into 114 *surahs* (chapters). It starts by saying that Allah is the one true god. Then it discusses Allah's role in history and Muhammad's role as Allah's prophet. The Qur'an describes Allah's last judgement on his people and the need to help other people. It tells Muslims how to behave, as well as how to treat other people and animals. However, not everything is covered by the Qur'an, so Muslims also study the *Sunnah*, too. This book contains accounts of the words and deeds of Muhammad and his close followers. The *Sunnah* helps Muslims to gain a clear understanding of the Qur'an. Muslim laws are taken from both the Qur'an and the *Sunnah*. These laws, known as the *Shari'ah*,

◀ PATHWAY TO ALLAH
Islamic law is known as the Shari'ah. *This is an Arabic word meaning a track that leads camels to a waterhole. In the same way, Muslims who obey the* Shari'ah *will be led to Allah. The* Shari'ah *guides Muslims on their faith and behaviour. It is taught in law schools, such as this one, throughout the Islamic world.*

THE SUFIS
Sufis are Muslims, who can be either Sunnis or Shi'ahs. They place complete obedience and trust in Allah. They try to get closer to Allah through dance and music. Sufi beliefs are passed down through the generations by saints and teachers. Many Sufis are involved in education and community work.

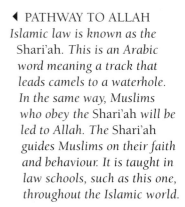

▶ SOULFUL SINGER
Sufis believe that music is both a path to Allah and a means of spiritual healing. They sing *qawwalis*, trance-like hypnotic songs that build up to an ecstatic climax. *Qawwali* singers such as Nusrat Fateh Ali Khan have achieved international fame.

▲ DERVISHES
Some Sufis dance and spin to forget the things around them and get closer to Allah. They are known as Whirling Dervishes.

▲ A SUFI
No one really knows how Sufis got their name. The word might come from *suf*, a basic woollen garment that early Sufis wore. Sufis turn their back on the world. They do not own many possessions and they often take vows of poverty.

provide detailed instructions to Muslims as to how to lead a good life. Sunni Muslims follow one of four different schools or interpretations of the *Shari'ah*. The Shi'ahs also follow the teachings of the first *imams*, the spiritual leaders descended from Ali, Muhammad's cousin. They follow the teachings of individual thinkers, too. The greatest thinkers are known as *ayatollahs* (signs of Allah).

◀ THE QUR'AN
The Qur'an was prepared in about AD650 by Uthman, the third successor to Muhammad. Muslims consider it to be the perfect word of Allah. Only Muslims who have been ceremonially washed can touch it.

▶ SHI'AH LEADER
Muslims interpret the Qur'an in different ways. Ayatollah Khomeini was leader of Iran between 1979 and 1989. He interpreted the Qur'an very strictly. During his decade of power, he applied its teachings to every aspect of political and social life in his country.

▼ QAWWALI SHRINE, DELHI
One of the main Sufi shrines, dedicated to the Sufi saint Nizamuddin Awliya, is in Delhi, India. Its community of *qawwali* singers trace their ancestors back to Amir Khusrau (1253–1325). He was the founder of *qawwali* music.

▲ THE SIMURG
Sufis use a mythical bird, the *simurg*, to symbolize their search for unity with Allah. Its name is Persian for '30 birds.' The *simurg's* multi-coloured feathers represent every other bird that there is.

The Islamic Year

The Islamic calendar has 12 lunar months, each with 29 or 30 days.

- Muharram is the first month.

- Muslims celebrate the birthday of Muhammad on the 12th day of Rabi'I, the third month.

- Ramadan is the ninth month, when Muslims fast during daylight hours.

- Id-ul-Fitr (the breaking of the fast) is celebrated at the start of Shawal, the tenth month.

- Dhul-Hijjah, the 12th month, is when Muslims make their *hajj* (pilgrimage) to Makkah.

Modern religions

THE MAJOR RELIGIONS of the world were all formed more than 1,350 years ago. New religions are still being founded today, as people seek fresh answers to the age-old questions about the meaning of life and our place in the world. Some new religions, such as the Baha'i faith, are born out of existing ones. Others, such as the Moonies, are created by a visionary leader, who starts a completely new faith. All new religions borrow elements from existing ones and add new ideas of their own.

Both Islam and Christianity have inspired new religions. The Baha'i faith began in Iran in 1844, when a Shi'ah Muslim, Siyyid Ali-Muhammad, announced he was a *Bab* (gate) through which Allah communicates with his people. He predicted that a new prophet would arrive to lead Allah's people. Baha'is believe that Baha'u'llah (1817–92) was that prophet. Baha'u'llah was persecuted throughout the Middle East. Eventually he was exiled to Acre, in what is now Israel. From there, the Baha'i faith has spread throughout the world.

Christianity produced the Mormons and the Jehovah's Witnesses. Both of these believe that the second coming of Jesus Christ is close, a belief shared

▲ MARY BAKER EDDY
Christian Scientists believe that illness can be cured by prayer and so believers do not take medicines or even accept blood transfusions. The religion was founded by the American Mary Baker Eddy (1821-1910).

▶ MORMONS
The Church of Jesus Christ of Latter-Day Saints are better known as the Mormons. Their name comes from the Book of Mormon, which their founder Joseph Smith (1805–44) claimed to have translated under God's guidance. Mormons believe the book is equal to the Old and New Testaments of the Bible. Here you can see the first Mormon church leaders.

RASTAFARIANISM
Rastafarians believe that they are the descendants of the 12 tribes of Israel. They worship the Hebrew God, whom they call Jah. They believe that the white world is godless, and that black people will eventually return to Africa to achieve their freedom. Their messiah, after whom they take their name, is Haile Selassie, the only black leader in Africa to keep his country independent of white, European rule.

◀ THE ETHIOPIAN FLAG
The green, yellow and red colours on the flag of Ethiopia have been adopted by Rastafarians as their own personal colours. They have also added black, which appears on the flag designed by Marcus Garvey.

◀ DREADLOCKS
Rastas wear their hair in dreadlocks. The style is inspired by the description in the Bible of the mane of the Lion of Judah. It is also an outward sign that Rastas refuse to conform to the expectations of white people.

▶ BLACK ACTIVIST
In 1914 Jamaican-born Marcus Garvey set up the Universal Negro Improvement Association. He urged black people to assert themselves and return to Africa. He said a Black Messiah would appear there to redeem (save) black people.

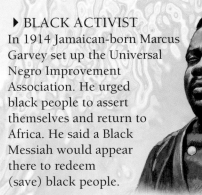

◄ THE MOONIES
The Unification Church was founded in Korea by Sun Myung Moon in 1954. The Moonies hold mass weddings, at which the couples are purified so that their children will be born without sin.

▲ THE RAELIANS
The UFO writer Claude Vorilhon formed the Raëlian cult in 1973. He also renamed himself Raël. Raëlians believe that one day extraterrestrials will land on Earth. According to Raël, these aliens are what we have mistaken for gods or God in all the world's religions. The Raëlian symbol represents star systems inside bigger star systems.

by the Seventh Day Adventists and other new Christian churches. Rastafarians believe in the Old Testament but worship a visionary leader, the Ethiopian emperor Haile Selassie.

Although all the new religions are very different, they often share two central beliefs. The first is the idea that a new messiah or prophet has arrived to lead the people. The second is that the end of the world is coming soon. New Christian religions also believe that Jesus Christ will return to lead the world for 1,000 years, a belief known as millennarianism. Members of cults such as Heaven's Gate try to speed up the process of the end of the world with mass suicides.

Whatever their beliefs and differences, the new religions show us that as long as there is suffering and cruelty in the world, people will continue to look for new ideas and beliefs that make sense of the world.

▼ THE BLACK MESSIAH
Haile Selassie (Might of the Trinity) was the emperor of Ethiopia from 1930 until 1974. He was also known as Prince Ras Tafari. Rastafarians believe that he was the Black Messiah prophesied in 1916 by the black Jamaican activist Marcus Garvey.

▲ BOB MARLEY
Reggae is a music style that grew up in Jamaica in the 1950s and 1960s. It gained worldwide fame through the singing of Bob Marley. Many reggae stars are rastas. They sing about their faith in their songs.

Key Dates

- 1830 Joseph Smith translates the *Book of Mormon*.
- 1863 Baha'u'llah declares that he is the new prophet.
- 1870s Charles Taze Russell forms the Jehovah's Witnesses.
- 1930–74 Haile Selassie (Ras Tafari) rules Ethiopia.
- 1954 L Ron Hubbard founds the Church of Scientology.
- 1954 Sun Myung Moon founds the Unification Church in Korea.
- 1977 Marshall Applewhite founds the Heaven's Gate cult.

Glossary

A

afterlife Life after death, often in another world, such as heaven or the underworld.

ancient world The period of time between the birth of the first civilizations (around 5000BC) and the end of the Roman Empire (in AD476).

anoint To dab oil on to a person as a sign that they are blessed or holy.

ascetic A person who practises self-discipline to achieve spirituality.

B

Bible, The The Christian holy book, divided into the Old and New Testaments, each containing many different individual books.

C

civilization A settled society that has developed writing, organized religion, trade, great architecture and a form of government.

classical world The period of the great civilizations of Greece, Rome, China and the Mayans, from about 700BC to AD1000.

commandment An instruction or law given by God to his people.

Guru Nanak, the founder of Sikhism

The ancient Egyptian Hall of Two Truths

covenant An agreement or contract between God and his people.

cult A society or group of believers that often meets in secret.

D

disciple Someone who follows and believes in a religious leader.

divine Relating or referring to God.

dynasty A ruling family of kings or emperors, where the throne passes down through the generations.

E

embalm To preserve a dead body with salts to prevent it decaying.

empire A large area made up of different lands or countries, ruled by one government or leader.

enlightenment A state of being aware of the true nature of human existence and how one can end suffering.

G

gospel One of the first four books of the New Testament in the Bible.

guru A spiritual teacher and leader.

I

immortal Describes someone who will live forever.

initiation A ceremony by which a person is introduced into a religion.

K

kingdom A country ruled over by a royal dynasty.

M

meditation: The act of sitting and thinking about something deeply.

messiah The person sent by God to save his people. The Jews believe God will send a messiah to save them. Christians believe that Jesus was that messiah.

St Andrew and St James were two of Jesus's first disciples

missionary A person who travels abroad to convert the local people to his or her own religion.

monastery A religious building where monks live.

monk A man who lives in a religious community. Monks vow to live a life of poverty and obey God.

Muslim A follower of Islam.

N

nirvana The state of supreme happiness and enlightenment achieved by escaping from the desires of the world.

O

orthodox Traditional. There are orthodox branches of both Judaism and Christianity.

P

persecution To oppress, punish or harm someone for their beliefs.

philosophy A set of beliefs and values held by a person or group of people.

pilgrimage A journey to a holy place by a religious follower.

Pope The head of the Roman Catholic Church, based in Rome.

prophet Someone through whom God speaks.

R

Reformation The reform of the Roman Catholic Church in the 1500s that led to the founding of the Protestant churches.

The Dome of the Rock is sacred to Jews, Christians and Muslims

reincarnation The belief that when a person dies, he or she will be reborn in another body.

religion A belief in a god, gods, or a supernatural power, who must be worshipped and obeyed.

ritual A ceremony in which the order of events, and the words used, rarely change over the years.

S

saint A Christian who lived a good life, showed great faith in God and performed miracles.

sect A small religious group that has split from the main religion.

scripture A religious or sacred book or piece of writing.

shrine A sacred building or place, often housing a holy object.

sin Wrong or bad things that people do against the will of God.

soul The spiritual part of a person that combines with the body to make a human being.

spirit A person or being without a body.

symbolism The representation of something by something else. A cross symbolizes Christianity.

T

tribe A group of people who are often related and share the same language and culture.

U

underworld The mythical region beneath the world's surface where dead people are said to live.

V

vision A mystical or religious experience when a person sees God or something supernatural.

A shaman contacts the spirit world

Index